Berlitz®

Dutch

phrase book & dictionary

Berlitz Publishing
New York   London   Singapore

Contacting the Editors
Every effort has been made to provide accurate information in this publication, but changes are inevitable. The publisher cannot be responsible for any resulting loss, inconvenience or injury. We would appreciate it if readers would call our attention to any errors or outdated information. We also welcome your suggestions; if you come across a relevant expression not in our phrase book, please contact us at: **comments@berlitzpublishing.com**

All Rights Reserved
© 2007 Berlitz Publishing/APA Publications (UK) Ltd.
Berlitz Trademark Reg. U.S. Patent Office and other countries. Marca Registrada. Used under license from Berlitz Investment Corporation.

Eleventh Printing: March 2013
Printed in China

Managing Editor: Kate Drynan
Editorial Assistant: Sophie Cooper
Translation: updated by Wordbank
Cover Design: Beverley Speight
Interior Design: Beverley Speight
Production Manager: Raj Trivedi
Picture Researcher: Beverley Speight
Cover Photo: © APA Julian Love

Interior Photos: APA Julian Love p.1,12, 56, 59; APA Britta Jaschinski p. 17, 77; APA Greg Gladman p.103, 127, 132, 140; APA Corrie Wingate p125; istockphoto p.14, 21,25,29,32,37,42, 45,48,63,65,69,74,79,100,104,108,117,119, 121,129,130,139,145,147,148,151,153,154, 157, 159,161; APA Lucy Johnston p.171.

Contents

Food & Drink

People

Leisure Time

Special Requirements

In an Emergency

Dictionary

Pronunciation

This section is designed to make you familiar with the sounds of Dutch by using our simplified phonetic transcription. You'll find the pronunciation of the Dutch letters and sounds explained below, together with their 'imitated' equivalents. This system is used throughout the phrase book: simply read the pronunciation as if it were English, noting any special rules below.

Stress has been indicated in the phonetic transcription with underlining. Dutch has many vowel sounds, and some may be unfamiliar to your ear. The best approximation is provided overleaf, but try to listen to Dutch speakers to begin to develop accuracy in pronunciation.

Dutch counts over 20 million speakers worldwide and is the principal language of Nederland (the Netherlands), often incorrectly referred to as Holland (North-Holland and South-Holland are Dutch provinces). Linguistically, Dutch is closely related to English and German, and you'll find that the majority of the population has at least basic knowledge of English. This shouldn't stop you from practicing your Dutch; your efforts will be greatly appreciated.

The Flemish dialect is an official language in België (Belgium). Though Dutch and Flemish differ somewhat in vocabulary and pronunciation, each is easily understood by speakers of the other. Both Belgium and the Netherlands use a common literary language, Standard Dutch.

Dutch is an official language in some of its current and former territories, such as the Netherlands Antilles and Suriname. Dutch is also the parent language of Afrikaans, one of South Africa's official languages.

Consonants

Letter	Approximate Pronunciation	Symbol	Example	Pronunciation
ch	ch as in loch	**kh**	**nacht**	*nahkht*
d	1. as in English	**d**	**dag**	*dahkh*
	2. t as in cat, if at the end of a word	**t**	**bed**	*beht*
g	ch as in loch	**kh**	**groot**	*khroat*
j	y as in yes	**y**	**ja**	*yaa*
r	r as in ran, but rolled	**r**	**rijst**	*riest*
s	always hard as in pass	**s**	**stop**	*stohp*
sch	s followed by ch, as in loch	**skh**	**schrijven**	*skhrie·vuhn*
v	f as in fan	**f**	**vader**	*faa·duhr*
w	v as in van	**v**	**water**	*vaa·tuhr*

Letters b, c, f, h, k, l, m, n, p, q, t, x, y, z are generally pronounced as in English.

Vowels

Letter	Approximate Pronunciation	Symbol	Example	Pronunciation
a	a as in father	**ah**	**nacht**	*nahkht*
aa	aa as in aardvark	**aa**	**maar**	*maar*
e	1. e as in red	**eh**	**bed**	*beht*
	2. u as in up	**uh**	**meneer**	*muh·nayr*
ë	u as in up	**uh**	**drieën**	*dree·yuhn*
ee	ay as in hay	**ay**	**nee**	*nay*
i	1. i as in bit	**ih**	**kin**	*kihnt*
	2. ee as in seen	**ee**	**mini**	*mee·nee*

o	o as in not	**oh**	**pot**	*poht*
oo	oa as in boat	**oa**	**roos**	*roas*
u	1. u as in up	**uh**	**bus**	*buhs*
	2. ew as in new	**ew**	nu	**new**
uu	ew as in new	**ew**	**duur**	*dewr*

Vowel Combinations

Letter	Approximate Pronunciation	Symbol	Example	Pronunciation
ie	ee as in seen	**ee**	**zien**	*zeen*
ei*	ie as in tie	**ie**	**klein**	*klien*
ij**	1. ie as in tie	**ie**	**wij**	*wie*
	2. u as in up	**uh**	**lelijk**	*lay•luhk*
oe	oo as in too	**oo**	**hoeveel**	*hoo•fayl*

Letter	Approximate Pronunciation	Symbol	Example	Pronunciation
ou, au	ow in now	**ow**	**koud**	*kowt*
			auto	*ow•toa*
eu	u as in murky	**u**	**deur**	*dur*
ui	aw as in awe	**aw**	**huis**	*haws*

* Called **korte ei** (short i).

** Called **lan**ge ij (long i).

How to use this Book

Sometimes you see two alternatives separated by a slash. Choose the one that's right for your situation.

ESSENTIAL

I'm on vacation/business.
Ik ben hier met vakantie/voor zaken.
ihk behn heer meht faa·kahn·see/foar zaa·kuhn

I'm going to...
Ik ga naar... *ihk khaa naar*

I'm staying at the...Hotel.
Ik logeer in Hotel...
ihk loa·zhayr ihn hoa·tehl

Words you may see are shown in YOU MAY SEE boxes.

YOU MAY SEE...

DOUANE	customs
BELASTINGVRIJE GOEDEREN	duty-free goods
AANGIFTE GOEDEREN	goods to declare

Any of the words or phrases listed can be plugged into the sentence below.

Tickets

Is there a discount for...?
Is er korting voor...? *is ehr kohr·tihng foar..*

children
kinderen *kihn·duh·ruhn*

students
studenten *stew·dehn·tuhn*

senior citizens
ouderen *ow·duh·ruhn*

tourists
toeristen *toe·ris·ten*

Dutch phrases appear in purple.

Read the simplified pronunciation as if it were English. For more on pronunciation, see page 7.

Personal

I'm in a relationship. **Ik heb een relatie.** ihk hehp uhn ray·laat·see
I'm widowed. **Ik ben weduwnaar m /weduwe f**
ihk behn vay·dew·naar/vay·dew·ah

Do you have children/ **Heeft u kinderen/kleinkinderen?**
grandchildren? hayft ew kihn·duh·ruhn/klien·kihn·duh·ruhn
For Numbers, see page 165.

Related phrases can be found by going to the page number indicated.

When different gender forms apply, the masculine form is followed by m; feminine by f

VVV, Vereniging voor Vreemdelingenverkeer (tourist information offices), are located throughout the Netherlands, and offer a number of services such as assisting in travel arrangements, providing information about attractions and cultural events, booking tickets and making reservations.

Information boxes contain relevant country, culture and language tips.

Expressions you may hear are shown in You May Hear boxes.

YOU MAY HEAR...

Ik spreek slechts weinig Engels. I only speak a little English.
ihk sprayk slehkhts vie·nihkh ehng·uhls

Color-coded side bars identify each section of the book.

Survival

Arrival & Departure

ESSENTIAL

I'm here on vacation [holiday]/business.	**Ik ben hier met vakantie/voor zaken.** *ihk behn heer meht faa•kahn•see/foar zaa•kuhn*
I'm going to…	**Ik ga naar…** *ihk khaa naar…*
I'm staying at the…Hotel.	**Ik logeer in Hotel…** *ihk loa•zhayr ihn hoa•tehl…*

YOU MAY HEAR…

Uw kaartje/paspoort, alstublieft.
ew kaart•yuh/pahs•poart ahls•tew•bleef

Your ticket/passport, please.

Wat is het doel van uw verblijf?
vaht ihs heht dool fahn ew fehr•blief

What's the purpose of your visit?

Waar logeert u? *vaar loa•zhayrt ew*

Where are you staying?

Hoe lang blijft u? *hoo lahng blieft ew*

How long are you staying?

Met wie bent u? *meht vee behnt ew*

Who are you with?

Border Control

I'm just passing through.	**Ik ben op doorreis.** *ihk behn ohp doar•ries*
I'd like to declare…	**Ik wil graag…aangeven.** *ihk vihl khraakh…aan•khay•fuhn*
I have nothing to declare.	**Ik heb niets aan te geven.** *ihk hehp neets aan tuh khay•fuhn*

YOU MAY HEAR...

Heeft u iets aan te geven?
hayft ew eets aan tuh khay•fuhn

Do you have anything to declare?

Hierover moet u accijns betalen.
heer•oa•fuhr moot ew ahk•siens buh•taa•luhn

You must pay duty on this.

Kunt u deze tas even openmaken?
kuhnt ew day•zuh tahs ay•fuhn oa• puhn maa•kuhn

Can you open this bag?

YOU MAY SEE...

DOUANE	customs
BELASTINGVRIJE GOEDEREN	duty-free goods
AANGIFTE GOEDEREN	goods to declare
NIETS AAN TE GEVEN	nothing to declare
PASPOORTCONTROLE	passport control
POLITIE	police

Money

ESSENTIAL

Where's…?	**Waar is…?** *vaar ihs…*
the ATM	**de geldautomaat** *duh khehlt·ow·toa·maat*
the bank	**de bank** *duh bahngk*
the currency exchange office	**het geldwisselkantoor** *heht khehlt·vihs·suhl·kahn·toar*
What time does the bank open/close?	**Hoe laat gaat de bank open/dicht?** *hoo laat khaat duh bahngk oa·puhn/dihkht*
I'd like to change some dollars/pounds into euros.	**Ik wil graag wat dollars/ponden in euro's omwisselen.** *ihk vihl khraakh vaht dohl·lahrs/pohn·duhn ihn u·roas ohm·vihs·suh·luhn*
I want to cash some traveler's checks [cheques].	**Ik wil wat reischeques verzilveren.** *ihk vihl vaht ries·shehks fuhr·zihl·fuhr·uhn*

15

At the Bank

Can I exchange foreign currency/get a cash advance here?	**Kan ik hier buitenlands geld wisselen/geld opnemen?** *kahn ihk heer baw·tuhn·lahnds khelt vih·suh·luhn/khelt op·nay·men*
What's the exchange rate?	**Wat is de wisselkoers?** *vaht ihs duh vih·suhl·koors*
How much commission do you charge?	**Hoeveel commissie berekent u?** *hoo·fayl kohm·mihs·see buh·ray·kuhnt ew*
I think there's a mistake.	**Ik denk dat er iets fout is gegaan.** *Ihk dehnk daht eets fowt is khuh·khaan*
I've lost my traveler's checks [cheques].	**Ik heb mijn reischeques verloren.** *ihk hehp mien ries·shehks fuhr·loa·ruhn*

My card was lost.	**Ik ben mijn kaart kwijt.** *ihk behn mien kaart kwiet*
My credit card has been stolen.	**Mijn creditcard is gestolen.** *mien kreh•diht•kahrt ihs khuh•stoa•luhn*
My card doesn't work.	**Mijn kaart doet het niet.** *mien kaart doot heht neet*
The ATM ate my card.	**De geldautomaat heeft mijn kaart ingeslikt.** *Deh khelt•ow•toa•maat hayft mien kaart in•khe•slikt*

For Numbers, see page 165.

YOU MAY SEE…

VOER UW PAS IN	insert card
STOP	cancel
CORR	clear
OK	enter
PIN	PIN
GELD OPNEMEN	withdraw funds
VAN BETAALREKENING	from checking [current] account
VAN SPAARREKENING	from savings account
KWITANTIE	receipt

Cash can be obtained from **geldautomaten** (ATMs), which are located throughout the Netherlands. Some debit cards (with the Cirrus, EC or Maestro logo) and most major credit cards are accepted. Be sure you know your PIN and whether it is compatible with European machines, which usually expect a four-digit, numeric code. ATMs offer good exchange rates, though there may be some hidden fees.
GWK (Grenswisselkantoren), a Dutch financial company, offers foreign exchange, international transfer and traveler's check services. Exchanging foreign currency in a bank is another option. Bank opening hours do vary, but most are open Tuesday to Friday from 9:00 a.m. to 4:00 p.m. and on Mondays from1:00 p.m.

YOU MAY SEE...

Dutch currency is the **euro**, divided into **cents**.
Bills: 5, 10, 20, 50, 100, 500 **euro**
Coins: 1, 2, 5, 10, 20, 50 **cents** and 1 and 2 **euro**

Getting Around

ESSENTIAL

How do I get to town?	**Hoe kom ik in de stad?**	*hoo kohm ihk ihn duh staht*
Where's…?	**Waar is…?**	*vaar ihs…*
the airport	**het vliegveld**	*heht fleekh•fehlt*
the train [railway] station	**het station**	*heht staa•shohn*
the bus station	**het busstation**	*heht buhs•staa•shohn*
the subway [underground] station	**het metrostation**	*heht may•troa•staa•shohn*
How far is it?	**Hoe ver is het?**	*hoo fehr ihs heht*
Where can I buy tickets?	**Waar kan ik kaartjes kopen?**	*vaar kahn ihk kaart•yuhs koa•puhn*
A one-way/ return-trip ticket.	**Enkeltje/Retourtje.**	*ehng•kuhl•tyuh/ruh•toor•tyuh*
How much?	**Hoeveel kost het?**	*hoo•fayl kohst heht*
Are there any discounts?	**Kan ik korting krijgen?**	*kahn ihk kohr•tihng krie•khuhn*
Which gate/line?	**Welke gate/lijn?**	*vehl•kuh gayt/lien*
Which platform?	**Welk spoor?**	*vehlk spoar*
Where can I get a taxi?	**Waar kan ik een taxi krijgen?**	*vaar kahn ihk uhn tahk•see krie•khuhn*
Could you take me to this address?	**Kunt u me naar dit adres brengen?**	*kuhnt ew muh naar diht ah•drehs brehng•uhn*
Where can I rent a car?	**Waar kan ik een auto huren?**	*vaar kahn ihk uhn ow•toa hew•ruhn*
Can I have a map?	**Heeft u een kaart voor mij?**	*hayft ew uhn kaart foar mie*

Tickets

When's…to Amsterdam?	**Wanneer vertrekt…naar Amsterdam?** *vah·nayr fuhr·trehkt …naar ahm·stuhr·dahm*
the (first) bus	**de (eerste) bus** *duh (ayr·stuh) buhs*
the (next) flight	**de (volgende) vlucht** *duh (fohl·khuhn·duh) fluhkht*
the (last) train	**de (laatste) trein** *duh (laat·stuh) trien*
Where do I buy a ticket?	**Waar kan ik een kaartje kopen?** *Vaar kahn ik ehn kaar·tje koa·pen*
One ticket/Two tickets, please.	**Eén kaartje/Twee kaartjes, alstublieft.** *ayn kaart·yuh/tway kaart·yuhs ahl·stew·bleeft*
For today/tomorrow.	**Voor vandaag/morgen.** *foar fahn·daakh/mohr·khuhn*
A one-way [single]/round-trip [return] ticket.	**Enkeltje/Retourtje.** *ehng·kuhl·tyuh/ruh·toor·tyuh*
A first-class/economy-class ticket.	**Kaartje eerste klas/tweede klas.** *kaart·yuh ayr·stuh klahs/tway·duh klahs*
How much?	**Hoeveel kost het?** *hoo·fayl kohst heht*
Is there a discount for…?	**Is er korting voor…?** *is ehr kohr·tihng foar…*
children	**kinderen** *kihn·duh·ruhn*
students	**studenten** *stew·dehn·tuhn*
senior citizens	**ouderen** *ow·duh·ruhn*
tourists	**toeristen** *toe·ris·ten*
The express bus/express train, please.	**De snelbus/sneltrein, alstublieft.** *Duh snehl·buhs/snehl·trien, ahls·tuh·bleeft*
The local bus/train, please.	**De locale bus/trein, alstublieft.** *Duh low·kah·leh buhs, ahls·tuh·bleeft.*
I have an e-ticket.	**Ik heb een e-ticket.** *ihk hehp uhn ee·tih·kuht*
Can I buy a ticket on the bus/train?	**Kan ik in de bus/trein een kaartje kopen?** *kahn ihk ihn duh buhs/trien uhn kaart·yuh koa·puhn*
I'd like to…my reservation.	**Ik wil graag mijn reservering…** *ihk vihl khraakh mien ray·zehr·vay·rihng…*

cancel	**annuleren** *ah·new·lay·ruhn*
change	**wijzigen** *vie·zih·khuhn*
confirm	**bevestigen** *buh·fehs·tih·khuhn*

For Days, see page 167.

Plane

Airport Transfer

How much is a taxi to the airport?	**Hoeveel kost een taxi naar het vliegveld?** *hoo·fayl kohst uhn tahk·see naar heht fleekh·fehlt*
To...Airport, please.	**Naar...Airport, alstublieft.** *naar...air·pohrt ahls·tew·bleeft*
My airline is...	**Ik vlieg met...** *ihk fleekh meht...*
My flight leaves at...	**Mijn vlucht vertrekt om...** *mien fluhkht fuhr·trehkt ohm...*
I'm in a rush.	**Ik heb haast.** *ihk hehp haast*
Can you take an alternate route?	**Kunt u een andere route nemen?** *kuhnt ew uhn ahn·duh·ruh roo·tuh nay·muhn*
Can you drive faster/slower?	**Kunt u sneller/langzamer rijden?** *kuhnt ew snehl·luhr/lahng·zaa·muhr rie·duhn*

For Time, see page 166.

YOU MAY HEAR...

Met welke luchtvaartmaatschappij vliegt u? *meht vehl·kuh luhkht·faart·maat·skhah·pie fleekht ew*	What airline are you flying?
Binnenlands of internationaal? *bih·nuhn·lahnds ohf ihn·tuhr·naat·shoh·naal*	Domestic or International?
Welke terminal? *vehl·kuh tuhr·mee·nahl*	What terminal?

YOU MAY SEE...

AANKOMST	arrivals
VERTREK	departures
BAGAGEAFHAALRUIMTE	baggage claim
VEILIGHEID	security
BINNENLANDSE VLUCHTEN	domestic flights
INTERNATIONALE VLUCHTEN	international flights
INCHECKBALIE	check-in desk
E-TICKET INCHECKEN	e-ticket check-in
VERTREKGATES	departure gates

Checking In

Where is check-in?	**Waar is de incheckbalie?**
	vaar ihs duh <u>ihn</u>•tshehk•<u>baa</u>•lee
My name is…	**Mijn naam is…** *mien naam ihs…*
I'm going to…	**Ik ga naar…** *ihk khaa naar…*
I have…	**Ik heb** *Ihk hehp…*
one suitcase	**een koffer** *ayn koh•fur*
two suitcases	**twee koffers** *tway koh•furs*

one piece of hand luggage	**een stuks handbagage** *ayn stuhks hahnt·ba·kha·jeh*
How much luggage is allowed?	**Hoeveel bagage is toegestaan?** *hoo·fayl baa·khaa·zhuh ihs too·guh·staan*
Is that pounds or kilos?	**Is dat in ponden of kilo's?** *is daht in pohn·duhn of kee·loas*
Which terminal/gate does flight…leave from?	**Van welke terminal/gate vertrekt vlucht…?** *fahn vehl·kuh terminal/gayt fuhr·trehkt fluhkht…*
I'd like a window/ an aisle seat.	**Ik wil graag een stoel bij het raam/aan het gangpad.** *ihk vihl khraakh uhn stool bie heht raam/ aan heht khahng·paht*
When do we leave/ arrive?	**Wanneer vertrekken/arriveren we?** *vah·nayr fuhr·trehk·kuhn/ahr·ree·vay·ruhn vuh*
Is there any delay on flight…?	**Heeft vlucht…vertraging?** *hayft fluhkht…fuhr·traa·khihng*
How late will it be?	**Hoeveel vertraging heeft hij?** *hoo·fayl fuhr·traa·khihng hayft hie*

Luggage

Where is/are…?	**Waar is/zijn…?** *vaar ihs/zien…*
the luggage carts [trolleys]	**de bagagewagentjes** *duh baa·khaa·zhuh·vaa·khuhn·tyuhs*
the luggage lockers	**de bagagekluisjes** *duh baa·khaa·zhuh·klaws·yuhs*
the baggage claim	**de bagageafhaalruimte** *duh baa·khaa·zhuh·ahf·haal·rawm·tuh*
I've lost my luggage.	**Ik ben mijn bagage kwijtgeraakt.** *ihk behn mien baa·khaa·zhuh kviet·khuh·raakt*
My luggage has been stolen.	**Mijn bagage is gestolen.** *mien baa·khaa·zhuh ihs khuh·stoa·luhn*
My suitcase was damaged.	**Mijn koffer is beschadigd.** *mien kohf·fuhr ihs buh·skhaa·dihkht*

YOU MAY HEAR...

De volgende! *duh fohl·gun·duh*

Next!

Uw ticket/paspoort, alstublieft.
ew tih·kuht/pahs·poart ahls·tew·bleeft

Your ticket/passport, please.

Hoeveel stuks bagage heeft u?
hoo·fayl stuhks baa·khaa·zhuh hayft ew?

How many pieces of luggage do you have?

U heeft overbagage. *ew hayft oa·fuhr·baa·khaa·zhuh*

You have excess luggage.

Dat is te zwaar/groot voor handbagage.
daht ihs tuh zwaar/khroat foar hahnt-baa-khaa-zhuh

That's too heavy/large for a carry-on [to carry on board].

Heeft u deze tassen zelf ingepakt?
hayft ew day·zuh tahs·suhn zehlf ihn·khuh·pahkt

Did you pack these bags yourself?

Heeft iemand iets aan u gegeven om mee te nemen? *hayft ee·mahnd eets aan ew khuh·khay·fuhn ohm may tuh nay·muhn*

Did anyone give you anything to carry?

Vlucht...is aan het boarden.
fluhkht...ihs aan heht boar·duhn

Now boarding flight...

Finding your Way

Where is...?	**Waar is...?** *vaar ihs...*
the currency exchange office	**het geldwisselkantoor** *heht khelt·vihs·suhl·kahn·toar*
the car hire	**het autoverhuurbedrijf** *heht ow·toa·fuhr·hewr·buh·drief*
the exit	**de uitgang** *duh awt·khahng*
the taxi stand [rank]	**de taxistandplaats** *duh tahk·see·stahnd·plaats*
Is there...into town?	**Rijdt er...naar de stad?** *riet ehr...naar duh staht*

a bus	**een bus** *uhn buhs*
a train	**een trein** *uhn trien*
a subway [underground]	**een metro** *uhn may·troa*

For Asking Directions, see page 34.

Train

How do I get to the train station?	**Hoe kom ik bij het station?** *hoo kohm ihk bie heht staa·shohn*
Is it far?	**Is het ver?** *ihs heht fehr*
Where is/are...?	**Waar is/zijn...?** *vaar ihs/zien...*
the ticket office	**het loket** *heht loa·keht*
the information desk	**de informatiebalie** *duh in·fohr·mah·tsee·bah·lee*
the luggage lockers	**de bagagekluisjes** *duh baa·khaa·zhuh·klaws·yuhs*
mthe platforms	**de sporen** *duh spoa·ruhn*
Can I have a schedule [timetable]?	**Mag ik een spoorwegboekje?** *mahkh ihk uhn spoar·vehkh·book·yuh*
How long is the trip [journey]?	**Hoe lang duurt de reis?** *hoo lahng dewrt duh ries*
Do I have to change trains?	**Moet ik overstappen?** *moot ihk oa·fuhr·stahp·puhn*
Is the train on time?	**Is de trein op tijd?** *is duh trien ohp tiet*

For Tickets, see page 19.

YOU MAY SEE...

PERRONS	platforms
INFORMATIE	information
RESERVERINGEN	reservations
WACHTKAMER	waiting room
AANKOMST	arrivals
VERTREK	departures

De Nederlandse Spoorwegen (Netherlands Railways)
offers three types of trains, which vary in how frequently they
stop. Most stations are centrally located and you'll discover that the
longest train trip within the Netherlands is only about three hours.
There are two or more tracks to a platform, and electronic display signs
will indicate which track a train will leave from.
For domestic as well as international travel, a number of discounts
are offered (group, children's, off-peak). Keep in mind that purchasing
round-trip tickets, day travel cards or other specialty passes (Holland
Rail, Summer Trip, Euro) is usually more economical than purchasing
single tickets. Tickets may be purchased from machines or ticket offices
in larger stations. There is a slight surcharge for tickets purchased at
the counter. Note that you cannot buy tickets once on board, and you
may be fined if you do not show a valid ticket.

Departures

Which platform does the train to… leave from?	**Van welk spoor vertrekt de trein naar…?** *fahn vehlk spoar fuhr·trehkt duh trien naar…*

Is this the right platform for...?	**Is dit het juiste spoor voor...?**
	ihs diht heht yaw•stuh spoar foar...
Where is platform...?	**Waar is spoor...?** *vaar ihs spoar...*
Where do I change for...?	**Waar stap ik over voor...?**
	vaar stahp ihk oa•fuhr foar

On Board

Can I open the window?	**Mag ik het raam openen?**
	mahkh ihk heht raam oa•peh•nehn
Is this seat taken?	**Is deze plaats bezet?** *ihs day•zuh plaats buh•zeht*
That's my seat.	**Dat is mijn plaats.** *daht ihs mien plaats*
Here's my reservation.	**Hier is mijn reservering.**
	heer is mayn ray•sehr•vay•rihng

YOU MAY HEAR...

Kaartjes, alstublieft.	Tickets, please.
kaart•yuhs als•tew•bleeft	
U moet overstappen in...	You have to change at...
ew moot oa•fuhr•stahp•puhn ihn...	
Volgende halte is...	Next stop...
fohl•guhn•duh hahl•tuh ihs...	

Bus

Where's the bus station?	**Waar is het busstation?**
	vaar ihs heht buhs•staa•shohn
How far is it?	**Hoe ver is het?** *hoo fehr ihs heht*
How do I get to...?	**Hoe kom ik in...?** *hoo kohm ihk ihn...*

Is this the bus to…?	**Is dit de bus naar…?** *is diht duh buhs naar…?*
Does the bus stop at…?	**Stopt de bus bij…?** *stohpt duh buhs bie…*
Can you tell me when to get off?	**Kunt u me waarschuwen wanneer ik moet uitstappen?** *kuhnt ew muh* *vaar•skhew•vuhn vah•nayr ihk moot* *awt•stahp•puhn*
Do I have to change buses?	**Moet ik overstappen?** *moot ihk oa•fuhr•stahp•puhn*
Can you stop here, please?	**Kunt u hier stoppen, alstublieft?** *kuhnt ew heer stohp•puhn ahls•tew•bleeft*

For Tickets, see page 19.

For traveling short distances or for travel to destinations with no train service, taking the bus is a smart option. Service generally runs from around 6:00 a.m. until midnight. There are two types of bus tickets of interest to visitors: the **strippenkaart** (strip ticket) and the **dagkaart** (day ticket). The strip ticket is divided into strips (sold in divisions of 2, 3, 8, 15 and 45), which are used up as you cross zones. You always need one more strip than the number of zones you plan to travel. You can either stamp the ticket yourself or have the driver do it. Stamps are valid for at least an hour, so you can transfer to other buses, subways or trams, as long as you stay within the same number of zones. The day ticket might be more economical if you plan on making a lot of trips in a single day. For information on **excursies** (excursions) to classic tourist sights and for reservations, contact the **VVV, Vereniging voor Vreemdelingenverkeer** (tourist information office).

Metro

Where's the nearest metro [underground] station?	**Waar is het dichtstbijzijnde metrostation?** *vaar ihs heht dihkhtst•bie•zien•duh may•troa•staa•shohn*
Can I have a map of the metro [underground]?	**Mag ik een kaart van de metro?** *mahkh ihk uhn kaart fahn duh may•troa*
Which line for...?	**Welke lijn gaat naar...?** *vehl•kuh lien khaat naar...*
Which direction?	**Welke richting?** *vehl•keh rikh•tihng*
Where do I change for...?	**Waar stap ik over voor...?** *vaar stahp ihk oa•fuhr foar...*
Is this the right train for...?	**Is dit de juiste trein naar...?** *ihs diht duh yaw•stuh trien naar...*
Where are we?	**Waar zijn we?** *vaar zien vuh*

For Tickets, see page 19.

The **metro** [subway] operates from around 6.00 a.m. to midnight in and around Amsterdam and Rotterdam. You can use the **strippenkaart** (strip ticket) or buy a ticket from the automatic ticket machines. For the strip ticket, remember that you will always need one more strip than the number of zones you are going to travel. In Amsterdam, you also have the option of purchasing a **dagkaart** (day ticket), which offers unlimited travel on trams, buses, subways and canal buses.

Boat & Ferry

When is the ferry to…?	**Wanneer vertrekt de veerboot naar…?**
	vah•nayr fuhr•trehkt duh fayr•boat naar…
Can I take my car?	**Kan ik mijn auto meenemen?**
	kahn ihk mien ow•toa may•nay•muhn
What time is the next sailing?	**Wanneer vaart de volgende boot?**
	wah•nayr faart duh vohl•khehn•deh boat
Can I book a seat/ cabin?	**Kan ik een stoel/hut boeken?**
	kahn ihk uhn stool/huht book•ehn
How long is the crossing?	**Hoelang duurt de overtocht?**
	hoo•lahng dewrt duh oa•vehr•tohkht

For Tickets, see page 19.

YOU MAY SEE…

| **REDDINGSBOTEN** | life boats |
| **REDDINGSVESTEN** | life jackets |

There are a number of ferry companies with service to and from the Netherlands. Stena Line offers up to four sailings daily between **Hoek van Holland** (Hook of Holland) and Harwich, U.K. P&O Ferries sails between Rotterdam and Hull, U.K., while DFDS Seaways provides service from the Port of Ijmuiden in Amsterdam to Newcastle, U.K., up to seven times a week.

Inland ferries can also be taken to travel to **Waddeneilanden** (Frisian Islands), across **IJsselmeer** (IJssel Lake) and on many small rivers. Another option for water travel in Amsterdam is the canal bus; it offers regular service and stops that are located near the major museums, attractions and shopping areas. A **dagkaart** (day ticket) allows you to hop on and off as many times as you like until noon the next day. With this ticket you may also transfer to the metro or bus free of charge.

Taxi

Where can I get a taxi?	**Waar kan ik een taxi krijgen?**
	vaar kahn ihk uhn <u>tahk</u>•see <u>krie</u>•khuhn
Can you send a taxi?	**Kunt u een taxi sturen?**
	kuhnt ew uhn tahk•see stew•rehn
Do you have the number for a taxi?	**Heeft u het nummer voor een taxi?**
	hayft ew uhn nuh•mehr foor uhn tahk•see
I'd like a taxi for tomorrow at…	**Ik wil graag een taxi voor morgen om…uur.**
	ihk vihl khraakh uhn <u>tahk</u>•see foar <u>mohr</u>•khuhn ohm…ewr
Pick me up at…	**Haal me op om…** *haal muh ohp ohm…*
Can you take me to…?	**Kunt u me naar…brengen?**
	kuhnt ew muh naar…<u>brehng</u>•uhn
this address	**dit adres** *diht ah•<u>drehs</u>*

the airport	**het vliegveld** *heht fleekh•fehlt*
the train station	**het station** *heht staa•shohn*
I'm in a hurry.	**Ik heb haast.** *ihk hehp haast*
Can you drive faster/ slower?	**Kunt u sneller/langzamer rijden?** *kuhnt ew snehl•luhr/lahng•zaa•muhr rie•duhn*
Stop/Wait here.	**Stop/Wacht hier.** *stohp/vahkht heer*
How much?	**Hoeveel kost het?** *hoo•fayl kohst heht*
You said…euros.	**U zei…euro.** *ew zie…u•roa*
Keep the change.	**Houdt u het wisselgeld maar.** *howt ew heht vihs•suhl•khehlt maar*

For Numbers, see page 165.

For Numbers, see page 165.

YOU MAY HEAR…

Waar naartoe? *vaar naar too*	Where to?
Welk adres? *vehlk ah•drehs*	What's the address?
Er is een nacht/vluchthaventoeslag *ehr is uhn nahkht/fluhkht•haw• fehn•too•slahkh*	There's a nighttime/ airport surcharge.

Dutch taxis are marked by blue license plates and the word **TAXI** on the roof. Taxis should usually be booked in advance, rather than hailed in the street, though you might be able to hail one in larger cities. You can also go to a **taxistandplaats** (taxi stand). Tip by rounding up the fare.

There are also **water taxis** on the canals in Amsterdam.

Bicycle & Motorbike

I'd like to hire…	**Ik wil graag een…huren.**
	ihk vihl khraakh uhn… <u>hew</u>·ruhn
a bicycle	**fiets** *feets*
a moped	**brommer** <u>*brohm*</u>·*muhr*
a motorcycle	**motorfiets** <u>*moa*</u>·*tuhr*·*feets*
How much per day/ week?	**Hoeveel kost het per dag/week?**
	hoo·fayl kohst heht pehr dahkh/vayk

Cycling is very much a part of daily life in the Netherlands. Paths are marked with red and white signs or blue signs with a white bicycle for obligatory separate bike lanes.

Bikes may be rented at more than 100 train stations in the Netherlands. The daily rate is quite cheap, though you may have to leave a relatively high deposit. This will be returned when you bring the bike back in good condition.

You can take your bike on the train. There are a few things to remember though. You must purchase a ticket for your bike. It must travel in the special bike compartment. And you are not allowed to travel with bikes during rush hour.

| Can I have a helmet/lock? | **Mag ik een helm/slot?** *Mahkh ihk uhn hehlm/sloht* |

Car Hire

Where can I rent a car?	**Waar kan ik een auto huren?**
	vaar kahn ihk uhn <u>ow</u>•toa <u>hew</u>•ruhn
I'd like to hire...	**Ik wil graag...huren.** *ihk vihl khraakh...<u>hew</u>•ruhn*
a cheap/small car	**een goedkope/kleine auto**
	uhn khoot•<u>koa</u>•peh <u>ow</u>•toa
an automatic/	**een automaat/een handgeschakelde**
a manual	*uhn ow•toa•<u>maat</u>/uhn <u>hahnt</u>•kheh•<u>skhah</u>•kuhl•duh.*
a car with air	**een auto met airco** *uhn ow•toa meht air•coa*
conditioning	
a car seat	**een kinderzitje** *uhn <u>kihn</u>•duhr•ziht•yuh*
How much...?	**Hoeveel kost het...?** *<u>hoo</u>•fayl kohst heht...*
per day/week	**per dag/week** *pehr dahkh/vayk*
per kilometer	**per kilometer** *pehr <u>kee</u>•loa•may•tuhr*
for unlimited	**met onbeperkt aantal kilometers**
mileage	*meht ohn•buh•<u>pehrkt</u> aan•tahl <u>kee</u>•loa•may•tuhrs*
with insurance	**met verzekering** *meht fuhr•<u>zay</u>•kuh•rihng*
Are there any	**Zijn er ook kortingen voor...?**
discounts for...?	*zien ehr oak <u>kohr</u>•tihng•uhn foar...*

Fuel Station

Where's the next fuel station?	**Waar is het volgende benzinestation?**
	vaar ihs heht <u>fohl</u>•khuhn•duh behn•<u>zee</u>•nuh•staa•<u>shohn</u>
Fill it up, please.	**Vol, alstublieft.** *fohl ahls•tew•<u>bleeft</u>*
...liters, please.	**...liter, alstublieft.** *...<u>lee</u>•tuhr ahls•tew•<u>bleeft</u>*
I'd like to pay in cash/ by credit card.	**Ik wil graag contant/met een creditcard betalen.**
	ihk vihl khraakh kohn•<u>tahnt</u>/meht uhn <u>kreh</u>•diht•kaart buh•<u>taa</u>•luhn

YOU MAY HEAR...

Heeft u een internationaal rijbewijs?
hayft ew uhn ihn·tuhr·naat·shoo·naal rie·buh·wies

Do you have an international driver's license?

Mag ik uw paspoort zien, alstublieft?
mahkh ihk ew pahs·poart zeen ahls·tew·bleeft

Your passport, please.

Wilt u extra verzekering?
vihlt ew ehk·straa fuhr·zay·kuh·rihng

Do you want insurance?

U moet een borgsom betalen van...
ew moot uhn bohrkh·sohm buh·taa·luhn fahn...

There is a deposit of...

Kunt u hier even tekenen?
kuhnt ew heer ay·fuhn tay·kuh·nuhn

Can you sign here?

YOU MAY SEE...

BENZINE	gas [petrol]
LOODVRIJ	unleaded
NORMAAL	regular
SUPER	premium [super]
DIESEL	diesel

Asking Directions

Is this the right road to...?	**Is dit de juiste weg naar...?** *ihs diht duh yaw·stuh vehkh naar...*
How far is it to... from here?	**Hoe ver is het hiervandaan naar...?** *hoo fehr ihs heht heer·fahn·daan naar...*
Where's...?	**Waar vind ik...?** *vaar fihnt ihk...*

...Street	**de...straat** *duh...straat*
this address	**dit adres** *diht ah·drehs*
the highway [motorway]	**de snelweg** *duh snehl·vehkh*
Can you show me on the map?	**Kunt u dat op de kaart laten zien?** *kuhnt ew daht ohp duh kaart laa·tuhn zeen*
I'm lost.	**Ik ben verdwaald.** *ihk behn fuhr·dwaalt*

YOU MAY HEAR...

rechtdoor *rehkht·doar*	straight ahead
links *lihnks*	left
rechts *rehkhts*	right
op/om de hoek *ohp/ohm duh hook*	on/around the corner
tegenover *tay·khuhn·oa·fuhr*	opposite
achter *ahkh·tuhr*	behind
naast *naast*	next to
na *naa*	after
ten noorden/ten zuiden *tehn noar·duhn/tehn zaw·duhn*	north/south
ten oosten/ten westen *tehn oas·tuhn/tehn vehs·tuhn*	east/west
bij het stoplicht *bie heht stohp·lihkht*	at the traffic light
bij de kruising *bie deh kraw·sihng*	at the intersection

YOU MAY SEE...

STOP	stop
VOORRANG VERLENEN	yield
VERBODEN STIL TE STAAN	no standing

YOU MAY SEE...

	STOP	stop
	VOORRANG VERLENEN	yield
	VERBODEN STIL TE STAAN	no standing
	VERBODEN TE PARKEREN	no parking
	EENRICHTINGSVERKEER	one way
	VERBODEN IN TE RIJDEN	no entry
	VERBODEN IN TE HALEN	no passing
	VERBODEN TE KEREN	no U-turn
	AFSLAG	exit
	VOETGANGERSOVERSTEEKPLAATS	pedestrian crossing

Parking

Can I park here?	**Mag ik hier parkeren?**
	mahkh ihk heer pahr•kay•ruhn
Is there a parking lot [car park] nearby?	**Is er een parkeergarage in de buurt?**
	ihs ehr uhn pahr•kayr•khaa•raa•zhuh ihn duh bewrt
Where's...?	**Waar is...?** *wahr is...*
the parking garage	**de parkeergarage** *duh pahr•kayr•khah•raa•jeh*
the parking meter	**de parkeermeter** *duh pahr•kayr•may•tehr*

How much…?	**Hoeveel kost het…?** _hoo•fayl kohst heht…_
per hour	**per uur** _pehr ewr_
per day	**per dag** _pehr dahkh_
overnight	**per nacht** _pehr nahkht_

Breakdown & Repair

My car broke down.	**Ik heb autopech.** _ihk hehp ow•toa•pehkh_
My car won't start.	**Mijn auto wil niet starten.**
	mien ow•toa vihl neet stahr•tuhn
Can you fix it?	**Kunt u hem repareren?**
	kuhnt ew hehm ray•paa•ray•ruhn
When will it be ready?	**Wanneer is hij klaar?** _vahn•nayr ihs hie klaar_
How much?	**Hoeveel kost het?** _hoo•fayl kohst heht_
I have a puncture/	**Ik heb een lek/lekke band**
flat tyre (tire).	_ik hehp ayn leh•keh bahnt_

Accidents

There's been an	**Er is een ongeluk gebeurd.**
accident.	_ehr ihs uhn ohn•khuh•luhk khuh•burt_
Call an ambulance/	**Bel een ambulance/de politie.**
the police.	_bel uhn ahm•bew•lahn•suh/duh poa•leet•see_

Places to Stay

ESSENTIAL

Can you recommend a hotel?	**Kunt u een hotel aanbevelen?** *kuhnt ew uhn hoa·tehl aan·buh·fay·luhn*
I have a reservation.	**Ik heb een reservering.** *ihk hehp uhn ray·zuhr·vay·rihng*
My name is…	**Mijn naam is…** *mien naam ihs…*
Do you have a room…?	**Heeft u een kamer…?** *hayft ew uhn kaa·muhr…*
for one	**voor één persoon** *foar ayn puhr·soan*
Do you have a room…?	**Heeft u een kamer…?** *hayft ew uhn kaa·muhr…*
for two	**voor twee personen** *foar tvay puhr·soa·nuhn*
with a bathroom [toilet]/shower	**met toilet/douche** *meht twaa·leht/doosh*
with air conditioning	**met airco** *meht air·coa*
For tonight.	**Voor vannacht.** *foar fahn·nahkht*
For two nights.	**Voor twee nachten.** *foar tvay nahkh·tuhn*
For one week.	**Voor één week.** *foar ayn vayk*
How much?	**Hoeveel kost het?** *hoo·fayl kohst heht*
Do you have anything cheaper?	**Heeft u iets goedkopers?** *hayft ew eets khoot·koa·puhrs*
When's check-out?	**Hoe laat moeten we uitchecken?** *hoo laat moo·tuhn vie awt·check·uhn*
Can I leave this in the safe?	**Mag ik dit in de kluis bewaren?** *mahkh ihk diht ihn duh klaws buh·waa·ruhn*
Can we leave our bags?	**Mogen we onze bagage hier laten staan?** *moa·khuhn wie ohn·zuh baa·khaa·zhuh heer laa·tuhn staan*

Can I have the bill/ a receipt?	**Mag ik de rekening/een kwitantie?**
	mahkh ihk duh ray·kuh·nihng/uhn kvee·tahnt·see
I'll pay in cash/by credit card.	**Ik wil graag contant/met een creditcard betalen.** *ihk vihl khraakh kohn·tahnt/meht uhn kreh·diht·kaart buh·taa·luhn*

Somewhere to Stay

Can you recommend a hotel?	**Kunt u een hotel aanbevelen?**
	kuhnt ew uhn hoa·tehl aan·buh·fay·luhn
Can you recommend...?	**Kunt u een ... aanbevelen?**
	kuhnt ew uhn ... aan·beh·fay·lehn
a hostel	**een jeugdherbe** *uhn yukht·hehr·behrkht*
a campsite	**een camping** *uhn kehm·ping*
a bed and breakfast	**logies met ontbijt** *loa·khees meht ont·biet*
What is it near?	**Waar ligt het bij in de buurt?**
	vaar lihkht heht bie ihn duh bewrt
How do I get there?	**Hoe kom ik er?** *hoo kohm ihk ehr*

At the Hotel

I have a reservation.	**Ik heb een reservering.** *ihk hehp uhn ray·zuhr·vay·rihng*
My name is...	**Mijn naam is...** *mien naam ihs...*
Do you have a room...?	**Heeft u een kamer...?**
	hayft ew uhn kaa·muhr...
with a bathroom [toilet]/shower	**met toilet/douche** *meht twaa·leht/doosh*
with air conditioning	**met airco** *meht air·coa*
that's smoking/ non-smoking	**voor rokers/niet-rokers** *foar roa·kuhrs/neet·roa·kuhrs*
For...	**Voor...** *foar*
tonight	**vannacht** *fahn·nahkht*

In the Netherlands, there are a variety of accommodation options in addition to hotels, which range from one to five stars. You could choose to stay in a bed and breakfast, a **motel** (motel) if you are traveling by car, a **jeugdherberg** (youth hostel) or in a **vakantiehuisje** (vacation house). **Vakantiehuisje** refers to any rented living space, such as vacation cottages, apartments or houseboats. You might also want to try one of the **Centre Parcs**, which are vacation villages.

Prices are generally given per room and include breakfast, service charges and taxes (but do not include the extra city tax in Amsterdam). Reservations can be made through the Netherlands Reservation Center, which is free, **VVV** tourist offices, which charge a fee, and **GWK (Grenswisselkantoren)** offices.

two nights	**twee nachten**	*tvay nahkh•tehn*
a week	**een week**	*uhn vayk*
Does the hotel have…?	**Heeft het hotel…?**	*hayft heht hoa•tehl…*
a computer	**een computer**	*uhn kohm•pyoo•tuhr*
an elevator [lift]	**een lift**	*uhn lihft*
(wireless) internet service	**(draadloze) internetverbinding**	*(draat•loa•zuh) ihn•tuhr•neht•fuhr•bihn•dihng*
room service	**roomservice**	*room•suhr•vihs*
a gym	**een fitnessruimte**	*uhn fiht•nehs•rawm•tuh*
a pool	**een zwembad**	*uhn swehm•baht*
I need…	**Ik wil…**	*ihk vihl…*
an extra bed	**een extra bed**	*uhn ehk•straa beht*
a cot	**een kinderbed**	*uhn kihn•duhr•beht*
a crib [child's cot]	**een wieg**	*uhn veekh*

YOU MAY HEAR...

Uw paspoort/creditcard, alstublieft.
ew pahs·poart/creditkaart ahls·tew·bleeft

Vul dit formulier in.
fuhl diht fohr·mew·leer ihn

Kunt u hier even tekenen?
kuhnt ew heer ay·fuhn tay·kuh·nuhn
ay·fuhn tay·kuh·nuhn

Your passport/credit card, please.

Fill out this form.

Can you sign here?

Price

How much per night/week?	**Hoeveel kost het per nacht/week?** *hoo·fayl kohst heht pehr nahkht/vayk*
Does the price include breakfast/sales tax [VAT]?	**Is het ontbijt/de BTW bij de prijs inbegrepen?** *lhs heht ohnt·biet/bay·tay·vay bie duh pries ihn·buh·khray·puhn*
Are there any discounts?	**Is er een korting?** *is ehr uhn kohr·ting*

Preferences

Can I see the room?	**Mag ik de kamer zien?** *mahkh ihk duh kaa·mehr seen*
I'd like a... room.	**Ik wil graag een... kamer.** *lhk vihl khraakh uhn... kaa·muhr*
better	**beter** *bay·ter*
bigger	**groter** *khroa·tehr*
cheaper	**goedkoper** *khoot·koa·pehr*
quieter	**stiller** *stih·lehr*
I'll take it.	**Ik neem hem** *ihk naym hehm*
No, I won't take it.	**Nee, ik neem hem niet.** *nay, ihk naym hehm neet*

Questions

Where's...?	**Waar is...?** *vaar ihs...*
the bar	**de bar** *duh bahr*
the bathroom [toilet]	**het toilet** *heht tvaa·leht*
the elevator [lift]	**de lift** *duh lihft*
Can I have...?	**Mag ik...?** *mahkh ihk...*
a blanket	**een deken** *uhn day·kuhn*
an iron	**een strijkijzer** *uhn striek·ie·zuhr*
a pillow	**een kussen** *uhn kuh·suhn*
the room key/ key card	**de kamersleutel/sleutelkaart** *duh kah·merh·slu·tehl/slu·tehl·kaart*
soap	**zeep** *zayp*
toilet paper	**toiletpapier** *tvaa·leht·paa·peer*
a towel	**een handdoek** *uhn hahn·dook*
Do you have an adapter for this?	**Heeft u hier een adapter voor?** *hayft ew heer uhn ah·dahp·tuhr foar*
How do I turn on the lights?	**Hoe doe ik het licht aan?** *hoo doo ihk heht lihkht aan*
Can you wake me at...?	**Kunt u me om...wakker maken?** *kuhnt ew muh ohm...vahk·kuhr maa·kuhn*

Can I have my things from the safe?	**Mag ik mijn spullen uit de kluis hebben?**
	mahkh ihk mien <u>spuh</u>·luhn awt duh klaws <u>heh</u>·buhn
Are there any messages for me?	**Zijn er berichten voor me?**
	zien ehr buh·<u>rihkh</u>·tuhn foar muh
Do you have a laundry service?	**Heeft u een wasserijservice?**
	hayft ew uhn <u>wahs</u>·seh·rie·ser·vice

YOU MAY SEE...

DUWEN/TREKKEN	push/pull
TOILET	bathroom [toilet]
DOUCHE	shower
LIFT	elevator [lift]
TRAP	stairs
VERKOOPAUTOMATEN	vending machines
IJS	ice
WASSERIJ	laundry
NIET STOREN	do not disturb
BRANDDEUR	fire door
NOODUITGANG/BRANDTRAP	emergency/fire exit
WEKDIENST	wake-up call

Problems

There's a problem.	**Ik heb een probleem.** *ihk hehp uhn <u>proa</u>·blaym*
I've lost my key/ key card.	**Ik heb mijn sleutel/sleutelkaart verloren.**
	ihk hehp mien <u>slu</u>·tuhl/<u>slu</u>·tuhl·kaart fuhr·<u>loa</u>·ruhn
I've locked myself out of my room.	**Ik heb mezelf buitengesloten.**
	ihk hehp muh·<u>zehlf baw</u>·tuhn·khuh·<u>sloa</u>·tuhn
There's no hot water/ toilet paper.	**Er is geen warm water/toiletpapier.**
	ehr ihs khayn vahrm <u>vaa</u>·tuhr/tvaa·<u>leht</u>·paa·peer

The room is dirty.	**De kamer is vies.**	*duh kaa•muhr ihs vees*
There are bugs in our room.	**Er zijn insecten op onze kamer.**	*ehr zien ihn•sehk•tuhn ohp ohn•zuh kaa•muhr*
...doesn't work.	**...doet het niet.**	*...doot heht neet*
Can you fix...?	**Kunt u...repareren?**	*kuhnt ew... ray•paa•ray•ruhn*
the air conditioning	**de airco**	*duh air•coa*
the fan	**de ventilator**	*duh fehn•tee•laa•tohr*
the heat [heating]	**de verwarming**	*duh fehr•vahr•mihng*
the light	**het licht**	*heht lihkht*
the TV	**de tv**	*duh tay•vay*
the toilet	**het toilet**	*heht tvaa•leht*
I'd like to move to another room.	**Ik wil graag een andere kamer.**	*ihk vihl khraakh uhn ahn•duh•ruh kaa•muhr*

Electricity in the Netherlands is 220 volts and sockets are for two-pin plugs. British and American appliances will need an adapter.

Checking Out

When's check-out?	**Hoe laat moeten we uitchecken?**
	hoo laat moo•tuhn vie awt•tshehk•kuhn
Can I leave my bags here until...?	**Mag ik mijn bagage hier laten staan tot...?** *mahkh ihk mien baa•khaa•zhuh heer laa•tuhn staan toht...*
Can I have an itemized bill/a receipt?	**Mag ik een gespecificeerde rekening/kwitantie?** *mahkh ihk uhn khuh•spay•see•fee•sayr•duh ray•kuh•nihng/kvee•tahnt•see*
I think there's a. mistake in this bill	**Ik geloof dat deze rekening niet klopt.** *ihk khuh•loaf daht day•zuh ray•kuh•nihng neet klohpt*
I'll pay in cash/by credit card.	**Ik wil graag contant/met een creditcard betalen.** *ihk vihl khraakh kohn•tahnt/meht uhn kreh•diht•kaart buh•taa•luhn*

Renting

I've reserved an apartment/a room.	**Ik heb een appartement/kamer gereserveerd.** *ihk hehp uhn ah•pahr•tuh•mehnt/kaa•muhr khuh•ray•zuhr•fayrt*
My name is…	**Mijn naam is…** *mien naam ihs…*
Can I have the key/ key card?	**Mag ik de sleutel/sleutelkaart?** *mahk ihk duh slu•tuhl/slu•tuhl•kaart*
Do you have…?	**Heeft u…?** *hayft ew…*
dishes	**serviesgoed** *sehr•vees•khoot*
pillows	**kussens** *kuh•suhns*
sheets	**lakens** *laa•kuhns*
towels	**handdoeken** *hahn•doo•kuhn*
kitchen utensils	**keukengerei** *ku•kehn•kheh•rie*
When/Where do I put out the bins/recycling?	**Wanneer/Waar moet ik recyclen/de vuilnis buiten zetten?** *vah•nayr/vaar moot ihk ree•sai•klehn/ duh vawl•nihs baw•tuhn zeht•tuhn*
…is broken.	**…is kapot.** *…ihs kaa•poht*
How does…work?	**Hoe werkt…?** *hoo vehrkt…*
the air conditioner	**de airco** *duh air•coa*
the dishwasher	**de afwasmachine** *duh ahf•vahs•maa•shee•nuh*
the freezer	**de diepvriezer** *duh deep•free•zuhr*

the heater	**de verwarming** *duh fuhr·vahr·mihng*
the microwave	**de magnetron** *duh mahkh·nuh·trohn*
the refrigerator	**de koelkast** *duh kool·kahst*
the stove	**het fornuis** *heht fohr·naws*
the washing machine	**de wasmachine** *duh vahs·maa·shee·nuh*

Domestic Items

I need...	**Ik heb...nodig.** *ihk hehp...noa·dihkh*
an adapter	**een adapter** *uhn aa·dahp·tuhr*
aluminum foil	**aluminiumfolie** *aa·loo·mee·nee·yuhm·foa·lee*
a bottle opener	**een flesopener** *uhn flehs·oa·puh·nuhr*
a broom	**seen bezem** *uhn bay·zuhm*
a can opener	**een blikopener** *uhn blihk·oa·puh·nuhr*
cleaning supplies	**schoonmaakmiddelen** *skhoan·maak·mih·duh·luhn*
a corkscrew	**een kurkentrekker** *uhn kuhr·kuhn·trehk·kuhr*
detergent	**waspoeder** *vahs·poo·duhr*
dishwashing liquid	**afwasmiddel** *ahf·vahs·mih·duhl*
bin bags	**vuilniszakken** *fawl·nihs·zah·kuhn*
a light bulb	**een gloeilamp** *uhn khlooy·lahmp*
matches	**lucifers** *lew·sih·fehrs*
a mop	**een dweil** *uhn dwiel*
napkins	**servetten** *sehr·feh·tuhn*
paper towels	**keukenpapier** *ku·kuhn·paa·peer*
plastic wrap [cling film]	**huishoudfolie** *haws·hout·foa·lee*
a plunger	**een ontstopper** *uhn ohnt·stoh·puhr*
scissors	**een schaar** *uhn skhaar*
a vacuum cleaner	**een stofzuiger** *uhn stohf·zaw·khurh*

For In the Kitchen, see page 73.

For Oven Temperature, see page 170.

At the Hostel

Do you have any places left for tonight?	**Heeft u nog plaatsen vrij voor vannacht?** *hayft ew nohkh plaat•suhn frie foar fahn•nahkht*
I'd like a single/ double room.	**Ik wil een eenpersoonskamer/ tweepersoonskamer.** *ihk wihl uhn ayn•pehr•soans•kahmehr/tvay•pehr•soans•kahmehr*
Can I have…?	**Mag ik…?** *mahkh ihk…*
a blanket	**een deken** *uhn day•kuhn*
a pillow	**een kussen** *uhn kuh•suhn*
sheets	**beddegoed** *beh•de•khood*
soap	**zeep** *zayp*
towels	**handdoeken** *hahn•doo•kuhn*
Do you have lockers?	**Heeft u kluisjes?** *hayft ew klaws•yehs*
What time do you lock up?	**Hoe laat sluit u?** *hoo laat slawt ew*
Do I need a membership card?	**Moet ik lid zijn?** *moot ihk liht sien*
Here's my international student card.	**Hier is mijn internationale studentenkaart.** *heer is mien in•tehr•na•syoa•naa•leh stew•dehn•tehn•kaart*

Known as **Stayokay**, the Dutch Youth Hostel Association operates some 30 official youth hostels around the Netherlands in buildings ranging from modern facilities to castles or country houses. You may request a private or shared room; breakfast and sheets are included in the price. Hostelling International (HI) cardholders are exempt from surcharges and receive special discounts. You may purchase HI cards on the spot. There are also a number of unofficial hostels throughout the country. The quality of these may range from poor to excellent.

Going Camping

Can we camp here?	**Mogen we hier kamperen?**
	moa·khuhn vie heer kahm·pay·ruhn
Is there a campsite near here?	**Is er een camping in de buurt?**
	ihs ehr uhn kehm·pihng ihn duh bewrt
What is the charge per day/week?	**Hoeveel kost het per dag/week?**
	hoo·fayl kohst heht pehr daakh/vayk
Do you have…?	**Heeft u…?** *hayft ew…*
cooking facilities	**kookgelegenheid** *koak·khuh·lay·khuhn·hiet*
electrical outlets	**stopcontacten** *stohp·kohn·tahk·tuhn*
laundry facilities	**wasmachines** *vahs·maa·shee·nuhs*
showers	**douches** *doo·shuhs*
tents for hire	**tenten te huur** *tehn·tuhn tuh hewr*
Where can I empty the chemical toilet?	**Waar kan ik het chemisch toilet legen?**
	vaar kahn ihk heht khay·mees tvaa·leht lay·khun

YOU MAY SEE…

DRINKWATER	drinking water
VERBODEN TE KAMPEREN	no camping
GEEN KAMPVUREN/BARBECUES	no fires/barbecues

ESSENTIAL

Where's an internet cafe?	**Waar vind ik een internetcafé?** *vaar fihnt ihk uhn <u>ihn</u>•tuhr•neht•kaa•<u>fay</u>*
Can I access the internet/check e-mail here?	**Kan ik hier internetten/mijn e-mail checken?** *kahn ihk heer ihn•tuhr•neh•tuhn/mien <u>ee</u>•mayl tsheh•kuhn*
How much per hour/half hour?	**Hoeveel kost het per uur/half uur?** *<u>hoo</u>•fayl kohst heht pehr ewr/hahlf ewr*
How do I connect/log on?	**Hoe kan ik verbinding maken/inloggen?** *hoo kahn ihk fuhr•<u>bihn</u>•dihng <u>maa</u>•kuhn/<u>ihn</u>•loh•khun*
I'd like a phone card, please.	**Ik wil een telefoonkaart, alstublieft.** *ihk vihl uhn tay•luh•<u>foan</u>•kaart ahls•tew•<u>bleeft</u>*
Can I have your phone number?	**Mag ik uw telefoonnummer?** *mahkh ihk ew tay•luh•<u>foan</u>•nuh•muhr*
Here's my number/e-mail address.	**Hier is mijn telefoonnummer/e-mailadres.** *heer ihs mien tay•luh•<u>foan</u>•nuh•muhr/<u>ee</u>•mayl•aa•<u>drehs</u>*
Call me.	**Bel me.** *behl muh*
E-mail me.	**Stuur me een e-mail.** *stewr muh uhn <u>ee</u>•mayl*
Hello. This is…	**Dag. U spreekt met…** *daakh ew spraykt meht…*
I'd like to speak to…	**Ik wil graag met…spreken.** *ihk vihl khraakh meht…<u>spray</u>•kuhn*
Can you repeat that?	**Kunt u dat herhalen?** *kuhnt ew daht hehr•<u>haa</u>•luhn*
I'll call back later.	**Ik bel straks wel even terug.** *ihk behl strahks vehl <u>ay</u>•fuhn truhkh*

Bye.	**Dag.** dahkh
Where's the post office?	**Waar is het postkantoor?**
	vaar ihs heht <u>pohst</u>•kahn•toar
I'd like to send this to…	**Ik wil dit versturen naar…**
	ihk vihl diht fuhr•<u>stew</u>•ruhn naar…

Online

Where's an internet cafe?	**Waar vind ik een internetcafé?**
	vaar fihnt ihk uhn <u>ihn</u>•tuhr•neht•kaa•<u>fay</u>
Does it have wireless internet?	**Is er draadloos internet?**
	ihs ehr <u>draat</u>•loas <u>ihn</u>•tuhr•neht
What is the WiFi password?	**Wat is het wifi-wachtwoord?**
	vaht is heht <u>wee</u>•fee <u>vahkht</u>•voart
Is the WiFi free?	**Is wifi gratis?** is wee•fee khrah•tis
Do you have bluetooth?	**Heeft u bluetooth?**
	hayft ew bluetooth
How do I turn the computer on/off?	**Hoe zet ik de computer aan/uit?**
	hoo zeht ihk duh kohm•<u>pyoo</u>•tuhr aan/awt
Can I…?	**Kan ik…?** kahn ihk…
access the internet here	**hier internetten** heer <u>ihn</u>•tuhr•neh•tuhn
check e-mail	**mijn e-mail checken** mien <u>ee</u>•mayl <u>tsheh</u>•kuhn
print	**printen** <u>prihn</u>•tuhn
plug in/charge my laptop/iPhone/iPad/BlackBerry?	**mijn laptop/iPhone/iPad/BlackBerry aansluiten/ opladen?** mien laptop/iPhone/iPad/BlackBerry <u>aan</u>•slaw•tehn/<u>ohp</u>•laa•dehn
access Skype?	**Skypen?** skypen
How much per hour/ half hour?	**Hoeveel kost het per uur/half uur?**
	<u>hoo</u>•fayl kohst heht pehr ewr/hahlf ewr
How do I…?	**Hoe moet ik…?** hoo moot ihk…

connect/disconnect	**verbinding maken/de verbinding verbreken**
	fuhr·bihn·dihng maa·kuhn/duh fuhr·bihn·dihng
	fuhr·bray·kuhn
log on/off	**inloggen/uitloggen** *ihn·lohkh·uhn/awt·lohkh·uhn*
type this symbol	**dit symbool typen** *diht sihm·boal tee·puhn*
What's your e-mail?	**Wat is uw e-mailadres?** *vaht ihs ew ee·mayl·aa·drehs*
My e-mail is…	**Mijn e-mailadres is…** *mien ee·mayl·aa·drehs ihs…*
Do you have a scanner?	**Heeft u een scanner?** *hayft ew uhn scanner*

Social Media

Are you on Facebook/ Twitter?	**Bent u op Facebook/Twitter?**
	Behnt ew ohp Facebook/Twitter
What's your user name?	**Wat is uw gebruikersnaam?**
	waht is ew kheh·braw·kehrs·naam
I'll add you as a friend.	**Ik zal u toevoegen als vriend.**
	ik sahl ew too·foo·khehn ahls freent
I'll follow you on Twitter.	**Ik zal u volgen op Twitter.**
	ik sahl ew fohl·khehn op twitter
Are you following…?	**Volgt u…?** *fohlkht ew*
I'll put the pictures on Facebook/Twitter.	**Ik zal de foto's op Facebook/Twitter zetten.**
	ihk sahl duh foa·toas op facebook/twitter seh·tehn
I'll tag you in the pictures.	**Ik zal u op de foto's taggen.**
	ihk sahl ew ohp duh foa·toas taggen.

Phone

A phone card, please.	**Een telefoonkaart, alstublieft.**
	uhn tay·luh·foan·kaart ahls·tew·bleeft
How much?	**Hoeveel kost het?** *hoo·fayl kohst heht*
Where's the pay phone?	**Waar is de telefooncel?**
	waar is duh tay·leh·foan·sehl
What's the area/ country code for…?	**Wat is het netnummer/landnummer van…?**
	vaht ihs heht neht·nuh·muhr/lahnt·nuh·muhr fahn…

What's the number for Information?	**Wat is het nummer van Inlichtingen?**
	vaht ihs heht nuh•muhr fahn ihn•likh•tihng•uhn
I'd like the number for...	**Ik zoek het nummer van...**
	ihk zook heht nuh•muhr fahn...
I'd like to call collect [reverse the charges].	**Ik wil een collect call maken.**
	ihk wihl ayn collect call maa•kehn
My phone doesn't work here.	**Mijn telefoon werkt hier niet.**
	mien tay•luh•foan vehrkt heer neet
What network are you on?	**Op welk netwerk zit u?**
	ohp vehlk neht•vehrk siht ew
Is it 3G?	**Is het 3G?** *is heht dree•khay*
I have run out of credit/minutes.	**Mijn tegoed/minuten zijn op.**
	mien tuh•khooht/meen•ew•tehn sien ohp
Can I buy some credit?	**Kan ik tegoed kopen?** *kahn ihk tuh•khooht koa•pehn*

YOU MAY SEE...

SLUITEN	close
VERWIJDEREN	delete
E-MAIL	e-mail
AFSLUITEN	exit
HELP	help
INSTANT MESSENGER	instant messenger
INTERNET	internet
INLOGGEN	login
NIEUW BERICHT	new message
AAN/UIT	on/off
OPENEN	open
AFDRUKKEN	print
VERZENDEN	send
GEBRUIKERSNAAM/WACHTWOORD	username/password
DRAADLOOS INTERNET	wireless internet

YOU MAY HEAR...

Met wie spreek ik? *meht vee sprayk ihk* — Who's calling?

Kunt u aan de lijn blijven? — Hold on.
kuhnt ew aan duh lien blie·fuhn

Hij?/Zij/is niet beschikbaar. — He/She can't come to the
hie?/zie/ihs neet buh·skhihk·baar — phone.

Wilt u een bericht achterlaten? — Would you like to leave a
vihlt ew uhn buh·rikht ahkh·tuhr·laa·tuhn — message?

Kan hij?/zij/u terugbellen? — Can he/she call you back?
kahn hie?/zie/ew truhkh·beh·luhn

Wat is uw nummer? *vaht ihs ew nuh·muhr* — What's your number?

Do you have a phone charger?	**Heeft u een telefoonoplader?** *hayft ew uhn tay·leh·foan·ohp·laa·duhr*
Can I have your number?	**Mag ik uw nummer?** *mahkh ihk ew nuh·muhr*
My number is…	**Mijn nummer is…** *mien nuh·muhr is…*
Please call me.	**Ik verzoek u me te bellen.** *ihk fuhr·zook ew muh tuh beh·luhn*
Please text me.	**Ik verzoek u me te sms'en.** *ihk fuhr·zook ew muh tuh ehs·ehm·ehs·uhn*
I'll call you.	**Ik zal u bellen.** *ihk zahl ew beh·luhn*
I'll text you.	**Ik zal u sms'en.** *ihk zahl ew ehs·ehm·ehs·uhn*

For Numbers, see page 165.

Telephone Etiquette

Hello. This is…	**Dag. U spreekt met…** *dahkh ew spraykt meht…*
I'd like to speak to…	**Ik wil graag met…spreken.** *ihk vihl khraakh meht… spray·kuhn*

Extension...	**Toestel...** _too·stehl..._
Can you speak louder /more slowly?	**Kunt u iets harder/langzamer spreken?**
	kuhnt ew eets hahr·duhr/lahng·zaa·muhr spray·kuhn
Can you repeat that?	**Kunt u dat herhalen?** _kuhnt ew daht hehr·haa·luhn_
I'll call back later.	**Ik bel straks wel even terug.**
	ihk behl strahks vehl ay·fuhn truhkh
Bye.	**Dag.** _dahkh_

For Business Travel, see page 141.

Fax

Can I send/receive a fax here?	**Kan ik hier een fax versturen/ontvangen?**
	kahn ihk heer uhn fahks fuhr·stew·ruhn/ ohnt·fahng·uhn
What's the fax number?	**Wat is het faxnummer?** _vaht ihs heht fahks·nuh·muhr_
Please fax this to...	**Kunt u dit faxen naar...** _kuhnt ew diht fahk·suhn naar..._

Post

| Where's the post office /mailbox [postbox]? | **Waar is het postkantoor/de brievenbus?** _vaar ihs heht pohst·kahn·toar/duh bree·fuhn·buhs_ |
| A stamp for this letter | **Een postzegel voor deze brief/ansichtkaart,** |

Postkantoren (post offices) can be recognized by the **TNT POST** sign. Regular offices are open Monday Friday from 9:00 a.m. to 5:00 p.m. Some larger ones are open on Saturday mornings. Stamps can often be bought from tobacconists, news kiosks and stationery shops. Mailboxes are orange. The mailbox has two slots, one for letters in the local area (the mailbox indicates which post codes go into this slot) and one for all other letters. The latter is marked **overige bestemmingen** (other destinations).

54

/postcard, please. **alstublieft.** *uhn pohst·zay·khuhl foar day·zuh breef/ahn·sihkht·kaart ahls·tew·bleeft*

How much? **Hoeveel kost het?** *hoo·fayl kohst heht*

I want to send this package by airmail /express. **Ik wil dit pakje per luchtpost/expres versturen.** *ihk vihl diht pahk·yuh pehr lukht·pohst/ehks·prehs fuhr·stew·ruhn*

Can I have a receipt? **Mag ik een kwitantie?** *mahkh ihk uhn kvee·tahnt·see*

YOU MAY HEAR...

Kunt u dit douaneaangifteformulier invullen? *kuhnt ew dit doo·aa·nuh·aan·khihf·tuh·fohr·mew·leer ihn·fuh·luhn*

Can you fill out the customs declaration form?

Hoeveel is dit waard? *hoo·fayl ihs diht vaart*

What's the value?

Wat zit hierin? *vaht ziht heer·ihn*

What's inside?

Public phones, mainly found in and around most train stations, are disappearing in the Netherlands due to the popularity of mobile phones. Public phones accept credit cards and **Telfort** phone cards, which may be purchased at all **NS** station ticket offices as well from **GWK** and some shops. Many public phones no longer accept coins. Schiphol Airport has added a new type of public phone, the **Multifoon** (multi-phone), that can be used to make calls, send e-mail and request information via the internet.

Important telephone numbers:

Emergencies 112 Operator assistance 0800 0410

To call the U.S. or Canada from the Netherlands or Belgium, dial 00 + 1 + area code + phone number. To call the U.K., dial 00 + 44 + area code (minus the first 0) + phone number.

Food & Drink

ESSENTIAL

Can you recommend a good restaurant/bar?	**Kunt u een goed restaurant/goede bar aanbevelen?** *kuhnt ew uhn khoot rehs•toa•_rahnt_/ khoo•duh bahr _aan_•buh•_fay_•luhn*
Is there a traditional Dutch/an inexpensive restaurant near here?	**Is er een traditioneel Nederlands goedkoop restaurant in de buurt?** *ihs ehr uhn traa•dee•shoa•_nayl_ nay•duhr•lahnds/ khoot•_koap_ rehs•toa•rahnt ihn duh bewrt*
A table for…, please.	**Een tafel voor…, alstublieft.** *uhn _taa_•fuhl foar… ahls•tew•_bleeft_*
Can we sit…?	**Kunnen we…zitten?** *_kuh_•nuhn vuh…_zih_•tuhn*
here/there	**hier/daar** *heer/daar*
outside	**buiten** *_baw_•tuhn*
in a non-smoking area	**in het gedeelte voor niet-rokers** *ihn heht khuh•_dayl_•tuh foar neet•_roa_•kuhrs*
I'm waiting for someone.	**Ik wacht op iemand.** *ihk vahkht ohp _ee_•mahnt*
Where are the toilets?	**Waar is het toilet?** *vaar ihs heht tvaa•_leht_*
Can I have a menu, please?	**Mag ik een menukaart, alstublieft?** *mahkh ihk uhn muh•_new_•_kaart_ ahls•tew•_bleeft_*
What do you recommend?	**Wat kunt u aanbevelen?** *vaht kuhnt ew _aan_•buh•_fay_•luhn*
I'd like…	**Ik wil graag…** *ihk vihl khraakh…*
Some more…, please.	**Nog wat…, alstublieft.** *nohkh vaht… ahls•tew•_bleeft_*
Enjoy your meal.	**Eet smakelijk.** *ayt _smaa_•kuh•luhk*

Can I have the check [bill]?	**Mag ik de rekening?**
	mahkh ihk duh ray·kuh·nihng
Is service included?	**Is de bediening inbegrepen?**
	ihs duh buh·dee·nihng ihn·buh·khray·puhn
Can I pay by credit card?	**Kan ik met een creditcard betalen?**
	kahn ihk meht uhn khreh·diht·kaart buh·taa·luhn
Can I have a receipt, please?	**Mag ik een kwitantie, alstublieft?**
	mahkh ihk uhn kvee·tahnt·see ahls·tew·bleeft
Thank you.	**Dank u.** *dahngk ew*

For Communications, see page 49.

Where to Eat

Can you recommend...? through.	**Kunt u...aanbevelen?**
	kuhnt ew...aan·buh·fay·luhn
a restaurant	**een restaurant** *uhn rehs·toa·rahnt*
a bar	**een bar** *uhn bahr*
a cafe	**een café** *uhn kaa·fay*
a fast-food place	**een fastfoodrestaurant**
	uhn fahst·food·rehs·toa·rahnt
a cheap restaurant	**een goedkoop restaurant**
	uhn khoot·koap res·tow·rahnt
an expensive restaurant	**een duur restaurant**
	uhn dewr res·tow·rahnt
a restaurant with a good view	**een restaurant met een mooi uitzicht.**
	uhn res·tow·rahnt meht uhn moy awt·sihkht
an authentic/non-touristy restaurant	**een authentiek/niet-toeristisch restaurant.**
	uhn ow·tehn·teek/neet-too·rihs·tees res·tow·rahnt

Reservations & Preferences

I'd like to reserve a table...	**Ik wil graag een tafel reserveren...** *ihk vihl khraakh uhn <u>taa</u>•fuhl ray•zuhr•<u>fay</u>•ruhn...*
for two	**voor twee personen** *foar tvay puhr•<u>soa</u>•nuhn*
for this evening	**voor vanavond** *foar fah•<u>naa</u>•fohnt*
for tomorrow at...	**voor morgen om...** *foar <u>mohr</u>•khuhn ohm...*
A table for two, please.	**Een tafel voor twee personen, alstublieft.** *uhn <u>taa</u>•fuhl foar tvay puhr•<u>soa</u>•nuhn ahls•tew•<u>bleeft</u>*
We have a reservation.	**We hebben gereserveerd.** *vuh <u>heh</u>•buhn khuh•<u>ray</u>•zuhr•<u>fayrt</u>*
My name is...	**Mijn naam is...** *mien naam ihs...*
Can we sit...?	**Kunnen we ... zitten?** *kuh•nehn wuh ... <u>sih</u>•tehn?*
here/there	**hier/daar** *hier/daar*
outside	**buiten** *<u>baw</u>•tehn*
in a non-smoking area	**in een niet-rokers ruimte** *ihn uhn neet-<u>roa</u>•kuhrs*
by the window	**bij het raam** *bie heht raam*
in the shade	**in de schaduw** *ihn duh <u>skhaa</u>•dew*
in the sun	**in de zon** *ihn duh sohn*
Where are the toilets?	**Waar is het toilet?** *vaar ihs heht tvaa•<u>leht</u>*

YOU MAY HEAR...

Heeft u gereserveerd?
hayft ew khuh•ray•zuhr•fayrt

Do you have a reservation?

Voor hoeveel personen?
foar hoo•fayl puhr•soa•nuhn

How many?

Roken of niet-roken?
roa•kuhn ohf neet•roa•kuhn

Smoking or non-smoking?

Wilt u al bestellen?
vihlt ew ahl buh•steh•luhn

Are you ready to order?

Wat mag het zijn? *vaht mahkh heht zien*

What would you like?

Ik kan...aanbevelen.
ihk kahn...aan•buh•fay•luhn

I recommend...

Eet smakelijk. *ayt smaa•kuh•luk*

Enjoy your meal.

How to Order

Waiter/Waitress!	**Meneer/Mevrouw!** *muh•nayr/muh•frow*
We're ready to order.	**We willen graag bestellen.** *vuh vih•luhn khraakh buh•steh•luhn*
I'd like...	**Ik wil graag...** *ihk vihl khraakh...*
a bottle of...	**een fles...** *uhn flehs...*
a carafe of...	**een karaf...** *uhn kah•rahf...*
a glass of...	**een glas...** *uhn khlahs...*
Can I have a menu?	**Mag ik de menukaart?** *mahkh ihk duh muh•new•kaart*
Do you have...?	**Heeft u...?** *hayft ew...*
a menu in English	**een menukaart in het Engels** *uhn muh•new•kaart ihn heht ehng•uhls*

a fixed-price menu	**een vast menu**	uhn _fahst_ muh•_new_
a children's menu	**een kindermenu**	uhn _kihn_•duhr•muh•_new_
What do you recommend?	**Wat kunt u aanbevelen?**	vaht kuhn ew _aan_•buh•_fay_•luhn
What's this?	**Wat is dit?**	vaht ihs diht
What's in it?	**Wat zit erin?**	vaht ziht ehr•_ihn_
Is it spicy?	**Is het sterk gekruid?**	ihs heht stehrk kheh•_krawt_
I'd like...	**Ik wil graag...**	ihk vihl khraakh...
More..., please.	**Ik wil graag nog wat..., alstublieft.**	ihk vihl khraakh nohkh vaht... ahls•tew•_bleeft_
With/Without...	**Met/Zonder...**	meht/_zohn_•duhr...
I can't eat...	**Ik mag geen...eten.**	ihk mahkh khayn..._ay_•tuhn
rare	**kort gebakken**	kohrt khuh•_bah_•kuhn
medium	**medium**	_may_•dee•yuhm
well-done	**goed doorbakken**	khoot doar•_bah_•kuhn
It's to go [take away].	**Het is om mee te nemen.**	heht ihs ohm _may_ tuh _nay_•muhn

For Drinks, see page 76.

YOU MAY SEE...

COUVERT	cover charge
DAGSCHOTEL	menu of the day
BEDIENING (NIET) INBEGREPEN	service (not) included
SPECIALITEITEN	specials

61

Cooking Methods

baked	**gebakken** *khuh·bah·kuhn*
boiled	**gekookt** *khuh·koakt*
braised	**gesmoord** *khuh·smoart*
breaded	**gepaneerd** *khuh·pah·nayrt*
creamed	**met room bereid** *meht roam buh·riet*
diced	**in blokjes gesneden** *ihn blohk·yuhs khuh·snay·duhn*
fileted	**gefileerd** *khuh·fee·layrt*
fried	**gebakken** *khuh·bah·kuhn*
grilled	**gegrild** *khuh·khrihlt*
poached	**gepocheerd** *khuh·poa·shayrt*
roasted	**geroosterd** *khuh·roa·stuhrt*
sautéed	**gesauteerd** *khuh·sow·tayrt*
smoked	**gerookt** *khuh·roakt*
steamed	**gestoomd** *khuh·stoamt*
stewed	**gestoofd** *khuh·stoaft*
stuffed	**gevuld** *khuh·fuhlt*

Dietary Requirements

I'm diabetic/ a vegetarian.	**Ik ben suikerpatiënt/vegetariër.** *ihk behn saw·kuhr·paa·shehnt/fay·khuh·taa·ree·yuhr*
I'm lactose intolerant.	**Ik heb lactose-intolerantie.** *ihk hehp lahk·toa·suh·ihn·toh·luh·rahnt·see*
I'm vegetarian/vegan.	**Ik ben vegetariër/veganist.** *ihk behn fay·kheh·taa·rie·yehr/fay·khah·nihst*
I'm allergic to…	**Ik ben allergisch voor…** *ihk behn ah·lehr·gees foar…*
I can't eat…	**Ik mag geen…eten.** *ihk mahkh khayn…ay·tuhn*
dairy	**zuivel** *zaw·fuhl*
gluten	**gluten** *khlew·tuhn*

nuts	**noten**	_noa•tuhn_
pork	**varkensvlees**	_fahr•kuhns•flays_
shellfish	**schelpdieren**	_skhehlp•dee•ruhn_
spicy food	**pikante gerechten**	_pee•kahn•tuh khuh•rehkh•tuhn_
wheat	**tarwe**	_tahr•vuh_
Is it halal/kosher?	**Is het halal/koosjer?**	_ihs heht haa•lahl/koa•shur_
Do you have...?	**Heeft u...?**	_hayft ew..._
skimmed milk	**magere melk**	_mah•kheh•reh mehlk_
whole milk	**volle melk**	_foh•leh mehlk_
soya milk	**sojamelk**	_soa•yah mehlk_

Dining with Children

Do you have children's portions?	**Heeft u kinderporties?** _hayft ew kihn•duhr•pohr•sees_
Can I have a highchair?	**Mag ik een kinderstoel?** _mahkh ihk uhn kihn•duhr•stool_
Where can I feed/ change the baby?	**Waar kan ik de baby voeden/verschonen?** _vaar kahn ihk duh bay•bee foo•duhn/fuhr•skhoa•nuhn_
Can you warm this?	**Kunt u dit opwarmen?** _kuhnt ew diht ohp•vahr•muhn_

For Traveling with Children, see page 143.

How to Complain

How much longer will our food be?	**Hoe lang moeten we nog op het eten wachten?**
	hoo lang moo·tuhn vuh nokh ohp heht ay·tuhn vahkh·tuhn
We can't wait any longer.	**We kunnen niet langer wachten.**
	vuh kuh·nuhn neet lahng·uhr vahkh·tuhn
We're leaving.	**We gaan weg.**
	vuh khaan vehkh
I didn't order this.	**Dat heb ik niet besteld.**
	daht hehp ihk neet buh·stehlt
I ordered…	**Ik heb om…gevraagd.**
	ihk hehp ohm…khuh·fraakht
I can't eat this.	**Dit kan ik niet eten.**
	diht kahn ihk neet ay·tuhn
This is too…	**Dit is te…**
	diht ihs tuh…
cold/hot	**koud/heet**
	kowt/hayt
salty/spicy	**zout/pikant**
	zowt/pee·kahnt
tough/bland	**taai/flauw** *taay/flow*
This isn't clean/fresh.	**Dit is niet schoon/vers.**
	diht ihs neet skhoan/fehrs

Paying

Can I have check [bill]?	**Mag ik de rekening?**
	mahkh ihk duh ray·kuh·nihng
We'd like to pay separately.	**We willen graag apart betalen.**
	vuh vih·luhn khraakh aa·pahrt buh·taa·luhn
It's all together, please.	**Alles bij elkaar, alstublieft.**
	ah·luhs bie ehl·kaar ahls·tew·bleeft

Is service included?	**Is de bediening inbegrepen?**
	ihs duh buh•dee•nihng ihn•buh•khray•puhn
What's this amount for?	**Waar is dit bedrag voor?**
	vaar ihs diht buh•drakh foar
I didn't have that. I had…	**Dat heb ik niet gehad. Ik had…**
	daht hehp ihk neet khuh•haht ihk haht…
Can I pay by credit card?	**Kan ik met een creditcard betalen?**
	kahn ihk meht uhn khreh•diht•kaart buh•taa•luhn
Can I have an itemized bill/a receipt?	**Mag ik een gespecificeerde rekening/kwitantie?**
	mahkh ihk uhn khuh•spay•see•fee•sayr•duh ray•kuh•nihng/kvee•tahnt•see
That was a very good meal.	**Dat was een uitstekende maaltijd.**
	daht vahs uhn awt•stay•kuhn•duh maal•tiet
I've already paid.	**Ik heb al betaald** *ihk hehp ahl beh•taalt*

Sales tax and service charges are already calculated into restaurant bills. Leaving as much as 10% is customary and appreciated, but not necessary.

Meals & Cooking

Ontbijt (breakfast) is usually eaten between 7:00 and 10:00 a.m. and consists of coffee and toast with jam or **hagelslag** (chocolate sprinkles). **Lunch** (lunch) is served from noon to 2:00 p.m. It is usually a light meal involving bread or rolls with cheese and cold cuts. **Avondeten** (dinner) is from 6:00 to 8:00 p.m. and is the main meal of the day. It may include soup, potatoes, meat and vegetables, followed by dessert.

Breakfast

boter _boa_·tuhr	butter
brood _broat_	bread
broodje _broat_·yuh	roll
ei _ie_	egg
roerei _roor_·ie	scrambled egg
honing _hoa_·nihng	honey
jam _zhehm_	jam
koffie met/zonder melk	coffee with/without milk
koh·fee meht/_zohn_·duhr mehlk	
melk _mehlk_	milk
thee _tay_	tea
roggebrood _roh_·khuh·broat	rye bread
toast _toast_	toast
vruchtensap _fruhkh_·tuhn·sahp	fruit juice

Appetizers

gerookte paling	smoked eel
khuh·_roak_·tuh _paa_·lihng	

huzarensalade	potato, vegetables and meat
hew·zaa·ruhn·saa·laa·duh	with mayonnaise
mosselen *moh·suh·luhn*	mussels
nieuwe haring *neeew·vuh haa·rihng*	freshly caught, salt-cured
	herring
oester *oos·tuhr*	oyster
pasteitje *pahs·tie·tyuh*	pastry filled with meat or fish
Russisch ei *ruh·see·suh ie*	hard-boiled egg filled
	with mayonnaise
zure haring *zew·ruh haa·ring*	pickled herring

Soup

aardappelsoep *aar·dah·puhl·soop*	potato soup
aspergesoep *ahs·pehr·zhuh·soop*	asparagus soup
bouillon *boo·yohn*	broth
bruinebonensoep	bean soup
braw·nuh boa·nuhn soop	
erwtensoep *ehr·tuhn·soop*	famous thick Dutch pea soup
	with pig's knuckle, smoked
	sausage and bacon
gebonden soep *khuh·bohn·duhn soop*	cream soup
groentesoep (met balletjes)	vegetable soup
khroon·tuh·soop (meht bah·luh·tyuhs)	(with meatballs)
heldere soep *hehl·duh·ruh soop*	consommé
kippensoep *kih·puhn·soop*	chicken soup
koninginnensoep *koa·nihng·ih·nuhn·soop*	cream of chicken soup
ossenstaartsoep *oh·suhn·staart·soop*	oxtail soup
tomatensoep *toa·maa·tuhn·soop*	tomato soup
uiensoep *aw·yuhn·soop*	onion soup
vermicellisoep *vehr·mee·seh·lee·soop*	clear noodle soup
vissoep *fihs·soop*	fish soup

The Netherlands has a mild climate, though it is often cool and rains a lot, which may explain the heaviness of the food. A very famous traditional winter dish is **erwtensoep** (pea soup), made from peas, winter vegetables and chunks of sausage or ham. It is typically served with crusty bread.

In a good **erwtensoep** you should be able to stand your spoon upright.

Fish & Seafood

forel _foa·rehl_	trout
garnaal _khahr·naal_	shrimp [prawn]
gerookte paling _khuh·roak·tuh paa·lihng_	smoked eel
haring _haa·rihng_	herring [whitebait]
haringsalade _haa·rihng·saa·laa·duh_	salad of herring, potatoes, beets, apples, pickles and mayonnaise
inktvis _ihnkt·fihs_	squid
kabeljauw _kaa·buhl·yow_	cod
krab _krahp_	crab
kreeft _krayft_	lobster
makreel _maa·krayl_	mackerel
mossel _moh·suhl_	mussel
nieuwe haring _neeew·vuh haa·rihng_	freshly caught, salt-cured herring
octopus _ohk·toa·puhs_	octopus
oester _oos·tuhr_	oyster
paling _paa·lihng_	eel
sardientje _sahr·deen·tyuh_	sardine
schelvis _skhehl·fihs_	haddock
schol _skhol_	plaice

stokvisschotel _stohk_·fihs·_skhoa_·tuhl	stew of dried cod, potatoes, rice, onions
tong tohng	sole
tonijn toa·_nien_	tuna
schelpdier _skehlp_·deer	clam
zalm zahlm	salmon

Meat & Poultry

biefstuk _beef_·stuhk	steak
blinde vink _blihn_·duh _fihnk_	stuffed slices of veal
duif dawf	pigeon
eend aynt	duck
fazant faa·_sahnt_	pheasant
gans khahns	goose
haas haas	hare
jachtschotel _yahkht_·skhoa·tuhl	meat casserole with potatoes
kalfsvlees _kahlfs_·flays	veal
kalkoen kahl·_koon_	turkey
kip kihp	chicken
konijn koa·_nien_	rabbit
lamsvlees _lahms_·flays	lamb
parelhoen _paa_·ruhl·hoon	guinea fowl

piepkuiken _peep_·_kaw_·kuhn	spring chicken
rundvlees _ruhnt_·flays	beef
spek spehk	bacon
varkensvlees _fahr_·kuhns·flays	pork
wienerschnitzel _vee_·nuhr _shniht_·suhl	breaded veal chops
worst _vohrst_	sausage

Vegetables & Staples

aardappel _aar_·dah·puhl	potato
andijvie ahn·_die_·vee	endives
bietje _beet_·yuh	beetroot
bloemkool _bloom_·koal	cauliflower
champignon shahm·_pee_·yohn	mushroom
erwt ehrt	pea
knoflook _knohf_·loak	garlic
komkommer kohm·_kohm_·muhr	cucumber
kool koal	cabbage
kruiden _kraw_·duhn	herbs
paprika (rode/groene)	(red/green) pepper
paa·pree·kaa (_roa_·duh/_khroo_·nuh)	
pasta _pahs_·taa	pasta
raap raap	turnip
rabarber _raa_·bahr·buhr	rhubarb
rijst riest rice selderij _sehl_·duh·rie	celery
sla slaa	lettuce
sperziebonen _spehr_·see·_boa_·nuhn	green beans
stamppot van boerenkool	kale and potatoes, with
met rookworst _stahm_·poht fahn	smoked sausage
boo·ruhn·koal meht _roak_·vohrst	
ui aw	onion
witlof _viht_·lohf	Belgian endive

witte asperge (met saus)	white asparagus (with sauce)
vih·tuh ah·spehr·zhuh (meht sows)	
wortel *vohr·tuhl*	carrot
zuurkool *zewr·koal*	sauerkraut

Fruit

aardbei *aart·bie*	strawberry
ananas *ah·naa·nahs*	pineapple
appel *ah·puhl*	apple
banaan *baa·naan*	banana
braam *braam*	blackberry
druif *drawf*	grape
framboos *frahm·boas*	raspberry
granaatappel *khraa·naat·ah·puhl*	pomegranate
grapefruit *grayp·froot*	grapefruit
kers *kehrs*	cherry
mandarijn *mahn·daa·rien*	tangerine
mango *mahn·goa*	mango
meloen *muh·loon*	melon
nectarine *nehk·taa·ree·nuh*	nectarine
perzik *pehr·zihk*	peach
pruim *prawm*	plum
rode bes *roa·duh behs*	red currant
sinaasappel *see·naas·ah·puhl*	orange
watermeloen *vaa·tuhr·muh·loon*	watermelon

Cheese

Edammer kaas *ay·dah·muhr kaas*	Edam mild cheese
Friese nagelkaas	cheese from Friesland, made
free·suh naa·khuhl·kaas	with skimmed milk and cloves
geitenkaas *khie·tuhn·kaas*	goat's cheese
Goudse kaas *khowt·suh kaas*	famous Gouda cheese

komijnekaas *koa·mie·nuh·kaas*   mild, hard cheese with cumin seeds; also called **Leidse kaas**

Leerdammer kaas *layr·dah·muhr kaas*   sweet, nutty cheese
Maaslander kaas *maas·lahn·duhr kaas*   Gouda-like cheese

Dessert

appeltaart *ah·puhl·taart*	Dutch apple tart
chipolatapudding *shee·poa·laa·taa·puh·dihng*	pudding of eggs, biscuits and liqueur
gebak *khuh·bahk*	pastry or cake
Haagse bluf *haakh·suh bluhf*	whipped egg whites with currant sauce
kwarktaart *kvahrk·taart*	light cheesecake
pannenkoek *pah·nuhn·kook*	thin pancake
poffertje *poh·fuhr·tyuh*	tiny sugared pancake
vla *flaa*	custard
vruchtenvlaai *fruhkh·tuhn·flaay*	Limburg fruit flan
wafel *vaa·fuhl*	waffle

Sauces & Condiments

zout *zowt*	salt
peper *pay·puhr*	pepper
mosterd *moh·stehrt*	mustard
ketchup *keht·suhp*	ketchup

At the Market

Where are the carts [trolleys]/baskets?	**Waar staan de wagentjes/mandjes?** *vaar staan duh vaa·khun·tyuhs/mahnt·yuhs*
Where is/are…?	**Waar is/zijn…?** *vaar ihs/zien…*
I'd like some of that/those.	**Ik wil graag wat van dat/die.** *ihk vihl khraakh vaht fahn daht/dee*

In the Netherlands, you'll find many **pannenkoekhuisjes** (pancake restaurants), which offer entire menus of sweet and savory pancakes. A traditional combination is **spekpannenkoek met stroop** (with bacon and syrup), substantial enough for a whole meal! Though **pannenkoeken** tend to be thick, there is a very popular thin variety called **flensjes.**

Can I taste it?	**Mag ik het proeven?**	*mahkh ihk heht proo•fuhn*
I'd like...	**Ik wil graag...**	*ihk vihl khraakh...*
a kilo/half-kilo of...	**een kilo/pond...**	*uhn kee•loa/pohnt...*
a liter/half-liter of...	**een liter/halve liter...**	*uhn lee•tuhr/hahl•fuh lee•tuhr...*
a piece of...	**een stukje...**	*uhn stuhk•yuh...*
a slice of...	**een plakje...**	*uhn plahk•yuh...*
More/Less than that.	**Meer/Minder dan dat.**	*mayr/mihn•duhr dahn daht*
How much?	**Hoeveel kost het?**	*hoo•fayl kohst heht*
Where do I pay?	**Waar moet ik betalen?**	*vaar moot ihk buh•taa•luhn*
Can I have a bag?	**Mag ik een tas?**	*mahkh ihk uhn tahs*
I'm being helped.	**Ik word al geholpen.**	*ihk vohrt ahl khuh•hohl•puhn*

For On the Menu, see page 80. For Conversion Tables, see page 169.

In the Kitchen

bottle opener	**flesopener**	*flehs•oa•puh•nuhr*
bowls	**kommen**	*koh•muhn*
can opener	**blikopener**	*blihk•oa•puh•nuhr*
corkscrew	**kurkentrekker**	*kuhr•kuhn•treh•kuhr*
cups	**kopjes**	*kohp•yuhs*

Measurements in Europe are metric — and that applies to the weight of food too. If you tend to think in pounds and ounces, it's worth brushing up on what the metric equivalent is before you go shopping for fruit and veg in markets and supermarkets. Five hundred grams, or half a kilo, is a common quantity to order, and that converts to just over a pound (17.65 ounces, to be precise).

YOU MAY HEAR...

Kan ik u helpen? *kahn ihk ew hehl•puhn*　Can I help you?
Wat mag het zijn? *vaht mahkh heht zien*　What would you like?
Anders nog iets? *ahn•duhrs nokh eets*　Anything else?
Het kost…euro. *heht kohst…u•roa*　That's…euros.

Food in the Netherlands can be bought at large supermarket chains, small specialty shops or local markets. Markets are excellent places to purchase regional products and organic goods such as fruit and vegetables, meat and baked goods and many other items such as flowers and clothing.

forks　　　　**vorken** *fohr•kuhn*
frying pan　　**koekenpan** *koo•kuhn•pahn*
glasses　　　**glazen** *khlaa•zuhn*

knives	**messen** _meh•suhn_
measuring cup/	**maatbeker/maatlepel**
spoon	_maat•bay•kuhr/maat•lay•puhl_
napkins	**servetten** _sehr•feh•tuhn_
plates	**borden** _bohr•duhn_
pot	**pot** _poht_
saucepan	**steelpan** _stayl•pahn_
spatula	**spatel** _spaa•tuhl_
spoons	**lepels** _lay•puhls_

YOU MAY SEE...

NA OPENEN HOUDBAAR TOT...	best if used by...
CALORIEËN	calories
VETVRIJ	fat free
GEKOELD BEWAREN	keep refrigerated
KAN SPOREN VAN... BEVATTEN	may contain traces of...
GESCHIKT VOOR DE MAGNETRON	microwaveable
UITERSTE VERKOOPDATUM...	sell by...
GESCHIKT VOOR VEGETARIËRS	suitable for vegetarians

Drinks

ESSENTIAL

May I see the wine list/drink menu?	**Mag ik de wijnkaart/drankkaart zien?** *mahkh ihk duh <u>vien</u>•kaart/<u>drahnk</u>•kaart zeen*
What do you recommend?	**Wat kunt u aanbevelen?** *vaht kuhnt ew <u>aan</u>•buh•fay•luhn*
I'd like a bottle/glass of red/white wine.	**Ik wil graag een fles/glas rode/witte wijn.** *ihk vihl khraakh uhn flehs/khlahs <u>roa</u>•duh/<u>vih</u>•tuh vien*
May I have the house wine?	**Mag ik de huiswijn?** *mahkh ihk duh <u>haws</u>•vien*
Another bottle/glass, please.	**Nog een fles/glas, alstublieft.** *nohkh uhn flehs/khlahs ahls•tew•<u>bleeft</u>*
I'd like a local beer.	**Ik wil graag een lokaal biertje.** *ihk vihl khraakh uhn loa•<u>kaal</u> beer•tyuh*
Can I buy you a drink?	**Wilt u iets van me drinken?** *vihlt ew eets fahn muh <u>drihng</u>•kuhn*
Cheers!	**Proost!** *proast*
A coffee/tea, please.	**Een koffie/thee, alstublieft.** *uhn <u>koh</u>•fee/tay ahls•tew•<u>bleeft</u>*
With/Without milk.	**Met/Zonder melk.** *meht/<u>zohn</u>•duhr mehlk*
With sugar.	**Met suiker.** *meht <u>zaw</u>•kuhr*
With artificial sweetener.	**Met zoetjes.** *meht <u>zoo</u>•tyuhs*
..., please.	**..., alstublieft.** *... ahls•tew•<u>bleeft</u>*
Juice	**Een vruchtensap** *uhn <u>fruhkh</u>•tuhn•sahp*
Soda	**Een frisdrank** *uhn <u>frihs</u>•drahngk*
(Sparkling/Still) Water	**(Koolzuurhoudend/Koolzuurvrij) Water** *(<u>koal</u>•zewr•how•duhnt/<u>koal</u>•zewr•<u>frie</u>) <u>vaa</u>•tuhr*

Non-alcoholic Drinks

appelsap *ah·puhl·sahp*	apple juice
cola *koa·laa*	cola
chocomel *shoa·koa·mehl*	chocolate milk
frisdrank *frihs·drahngk*	soda
grapefruitsap *grayp·froot*	grapefruit juice
koffie *koh·fee*	coffee
limonade *lee·moa·naa·duh*	lemonade
mineraalwater *mee·nuh·raal·vaa·tuhr*	mineral water
sinaasappelsap *see·naas·ah·puhl*	orange juice
thee *tay*	tea
warme chocolademelk *vahr·muh shoa·koa·laa·duh·mehlk*	hot chocolate

Aperitifs, Cocktails & Liqueurs

advocaat *aht·foa·<u>kaat</u>*	famous Dutch egg liqueur
brandewijn <u>*brahn*</u>*·duh·vien*	Dutch brandy
cognac *kohn·<u>yahk</u>*	brandy
gin-tonic *zhihn·<u>toh</u>·nihk*	gin and tonic
jenever *yuh·<u>nay</u>·vuhr*	Dutch gin

oranjebitter oa·<u>rahn</u>·yuh·bih·tuhr	slightly bitter liqueur
whisky <u>vihs</u>·kee	whisky
wodka <u>vohd</u>·kaa	vodka

Een kopje koffie met gebak (a mid-morning coffee, accompanied by a pastry), is somewhat of a Dutch ritual. Coffee is usually brewed strong and may be drunk black, with a little **koffiemelk** (condensed milk) or **slagroom** (whipped cream). Tea is brewed weak and is usually drunk without milk, sometimes **met citroen** (with lemon). **Kruidenthee** (herb tea), such as mint tea, and English tea are also popular.

YOU MAY HEAR...

Mag ik u een drankje aanbieden?	Can I get you a drink?
mahkh ihk ew uhn <u>drangk</u>·yuh <u>aan</u>·bee·duhn	
Met melk/suiker? meht mehlk/<u>zaw</u>·kuhr	With milk/sugar?
Koolzuurhoudend/Koolzuurvrij water?	Sparkling/still water?
<u>koal</u>·zewr·<u>how</u>·duhnt/<u>koal</u>·zewr·<u>frie</u> <u>vaa</u>·tuhr	

The Dutch are internationally famous for p**ilsener** or **pils** (lager) beer. Brands like Amstel™, Heineken™ and Grolsch™ are sold around the world. In the Netherlands, beer might even be drunk as **aperitief** (an aperitif) or instead of a **borrel** (this is usually **jenever**, the Dutch equivalent of gin). In fact, a good beer is often more deeply appreciated than a good wine.

Beer

bier/pils *beer/pihls*	beer/lager
donker bier <u>*dohng*</u>·*kuhr beer*	dark beer
flessenbier <u>*fleh*</u>·*suhn·beer*	bottled beer
getapt bier *khuh·*<u>*tahpt*</u> *beer*	draft [draught] beer
licht bier *likht beer*	light beer
oud bruin *owt brawn*	'old brown': a dark, slightly sweet stout

Wine

droge <u>*droa*</u>·*khuh*	dry
huiswijn <u>*haws*</u>·*vien*	house wine
mousserende *moo·*<u>*say*</u>·*run·duh*	sparkling
rode <u>*roa*</u>·*duh*	red
rosé <u>*roa*</u>·*say*	blush [rosé]
wijn *vien*	wine
witte <u>*vih*</u>·*tuh*	white
zoete <u>*zoo*</u>·*tuh*	sweet
dessert wijn *deh·*<u>*seh*</u> *wien*	dessert wine

On the Menu

aalbes _aal·behs_ — red currant
aardappel _aar·dah·puhl_ — potato
aardappelpuree _aar·dah·puhl·pew·ray_ — mashed potato
aardappelsalade _aar·dah·puhl·saa·laa·duh_ — potato salad
aardappelsoep _aar·dah·puhl·soop_ — potato soup
aardbei _aart·bie_ — strawberry
abrikoos _aa·bree·koas_ — apricot
advocaat _aht·foa·kaat_ — egg liqueur
amandel _ah·mahn·duhl_ — almond
amandelgebak _ah·mahn·duhl·khuh·bahk_ — almond tart
Amsterdamse ui _ahm·stuhr·dahm·suh aw_ — pickled onion
ananas _ah·naa·nahs_ — pineapple
andijvie _ahn·die·vee_ — endive
andijviesla _ahn·die·vee·slaa_ — endive salad
anijs _aa·nies_ — aniseed
anijslikeur _aa·nies·lee·kur_ — aniseed liqueur
anijsmelk _aa·nies·mehlk_ — aniseed milk
ansjovis _ahn·shoa·fihs_ — anchovies
aperitief _aa·puh·ree·teef_ — aperitif
appel _ah·puhl_ — apple
appelbol _ah·puhl·bohl_ — apple dumpling
appelflap _ah·puhl·flahp_ — apple turnover
appelmoes _ah·puhl·moos_ — apple sauce
appeltaart _ah·puhl·taart_ — apple pie or tart
artisjok _ahr·tee·shohk_ — artichoke
asperge _ahs·pehr·zhuh_ — asparagus
aspergesoep _ahs·pehr·zhuh·soop_ — asparagus soup
aubergine _oa·behr·zhee·nuh_ — eggplant [aubergine]
augurk _ow·khuhrk_ — gherkin

avocado *aa·voa·<u>kaa</u>·doa* — avocado
baars *baars* — bass, perch
babyinktvis <u>*bay*</u>*·bee·<u>ihngkt</u>·fihs* — baby squid
babyoctopus <u>*bay*</u>*·bee·ohk·toa·puhs* — baby octopus
baguette <u>*baa*</u>*·geht* — French bread
bami <u>*baa*</u>*·mee* — Chinese or Indonesian noodles
bami goreng <u>*baa*</u>*·mee <u>khoa</u>·rehng* — fried Chinese or Indonesian noodles

banaan *baa·<u>naan</u>* — banana
banketletter *bahn·<u>keht</u>·leh·tuhr* — pastry in letter shape with almond filling

basilicum <u>*baa*</u>*·see·lee·kuhm* — basil
bataat <u>*baa*</u>*·taat* — sweet potato
bavarois <u>*baa*</u>*·vaar·vah* — Bavarian cream
beignet <u>*behn*</u>*·yay* — fritter
beschuit *buh·<u>skawt</u>* — Dutch toast
bes <u>*behs*</u> — berry
biefstuk <u>*beef*</u>*·stuhk* — pan-fried steak
biefstuk van de haas <u>*beef*</u>*·stuhk fahn duh haas* — porterhouse steak

bier *beer* — beer
bieslook <u>*bees*</u>*·loak* — chives
bietje <u>*beet*</u>*·yuh* — beet [beetroot]
biscuit *bihs·<u>kvee</u>* — biscuit
bitterbal <u>*bih*</u>*·tuhr·bahl* — breaded meatball
bladerdeeg <u>*blaa*</u>*·duhr·daykh* — puff pastry
blauwe druif <u>*blow*</u>*·uh drawf* — red grape
bleekselderij <u>*blayk*</u>*·sehl·duh·rie* — celery
blikgroente <u>*blihk*</u>*·khroon·tuh* — canned vegetable
blinde vink <u>*blihn*</u>*·duh fihnk* — beef or veal meat roll
bloedworst <u>*bloot*</u>*·wohrst* — black pudding

bloem *bloom*	flour
bloemkool *bloom·koal*	cauliflower
boerenjongens *boo·ruhn·yohng·uhns*	brandy with raisins
boerenkool *boo·ruhn·koal*	kale
boerenmeisjes *boo·ruhn·mies·yuhs*	brandy with apricots
boerenomelet *boo·ruhn·oh·muh·leht*	omelet with potatoes, vegetables and bacon
bonen *boa·nuhn*	beans
borrel *boh·ruhl*	aperitif
borreltje *boh·ruhl·tyuh*	alcoholic drink
borst *bohrst*	breast
bosbes *bohs·behs*	blueberry
boter *boa·tuhr*	butter
boterbabbelaar *boa·tuhr·bah·buh·laar*	butterscotch
boterboon *boa·tuhr·boan*	butter bean
boterkoek *boa·tuhr·kook*	butter cookie [biscuit]
bouillon *boo·yohn*	broth
bourbon *bur·buhn*	bourbon
bout *bowt*	leg (cut of meat)
bowl *boal*	punch
braadstuk *braat·stuhk*	roast
braam *braam*	blackberry
brandewijn *brahn·duh·vien*	brandy
brasem *braa·suhm*	bream
brood *broat*	bread
broodje *broat·yuh*	bun, roll
broodkruimels *broat·kraw·muhls*	breadcrumbs
bruine boon *braw·nuh boan*	brown bean
bruinebonensoep *braw·nuh·boa·nuhn·soop*	brown bean soup
caffeïnevrij *kaa·fay·ee·nuh·frie*	decaffeinated
cake *kayk*	cake, sponge cake

caramelpudding *kaa•raa•mehl•puh•dihng* — caramel pudding
champignon *shahm•pee•yohn* — mushroom
cantharel *kahn•tah•rehl* — chanterelle mushroom
cantharellensoep *kahn•tah•reh•luhn•soop* — chanterelle mushroom soup
chipolatapudding *shee•poa•laa•taa•puh•dihng* — pudding of eggs, cookies [biscuits] and liqueur
chocolade *shoa•koa•laa•duh* — chocolate
chocomel *shoa•koa•mehl* — chocolate milk
citroen *see•troon* — lemon
citroengras *see•troon•khrahs* — lemongrass
citroensap *see•troon•sahp* — lemon juice
cognac *kohn•yahk* — brandy
consommé *kohn•soh•may* — consommé
cornflakes *kohrn•flayks* — cereal
courgette *koor•zheht* — zucchini [courgette]
dadels *daa•duhls* — dates
dagschotel *dahkh•skhoa•tuhl* — dish of the day
dessert/toetje *deh•sehrt/toot•yuh* — dessert
dessertwijn *deh•sehrt•vien* — dessert wine
dille *dih•luh* — dill
diner/avondeten *dee•nay/aa•fohnt•ay•tuhn* — dinner
donut *doa•nuht* — doughnut
dooier *doa•yuhr* — egg yolk
doperwt *dohp•ehrt* — garden pea
dragon *draa•khohn* — tarragon
drilpudding *drihl•puh•dihng* — jelly
druif *drawf* — grape
duif *dawf* — pigeon
Edammer kaas *ay•dah•muhr kaas* — Edam cheese
eekhoorntjesbrood *ayk•hoarn•tyuhs•broat* — porcini mushroom
eend *aynt* — duck

eidooier *ie·doa·yuhr*	egg yolk
eieren *ie·yuh·ruhn*	eggs
eiergerecht *ie·yuhr·khuh·rehkht*	egg dish
eigengemaakt *ie·khuhn·khuh·maakt*	homemade
eiwit *ie·wiht*	egg white
entrecote *ahn·truh·coat*	sirloin steak
erwt *ehrt*	pea
erwtensoep *ehr·tuhn·soop*	pea soup
fazant *faa·zahnt*	pheasant
filet *fee·lay*	fillet
flensje *flehns·yuh*	thin, small pancake
flessenbier *fleh·suhn·beer*	bottled beer
foelie *foo·lee*	mace (spice)
forel *foa·rehl*	trout
framboos *frahm·boas*	raspberry
fricandeau *free·kahn·doa*	meat with sauce
Friese nagelkaas *free·suh naa·khuhl·kaas*	cheese with cloves
frisdrank *frihs·drahngk*	soda
gadogado *khaa·doa·khaa·doa*	Indonesian mixture of vegetables, cucumber and tofu
gans *khahns*	goose
garnaal *khahr·naal*	shrimp [prawn]
garnering *khar·nay·rihng*	garnish, trimming
gebak *khuh·bahk*	pastry
gebakken kip *khuh·bah·kuhn kihp*	fried chicken
gebonden soep *khuh·bohn·duhn*	cream soup
gedroogde dadels *khuh·droakh·duh daa·duhls*	dried dates
gedroogde pruimen *khuh·droakh·duh praw·muhn*	dried prunes
gedroogde vijgen *khuh·droakh·duh fiekhuhn*	dried figs

gegrilde kip khuh·<u>khrihl</u>·duh kihp	grilled chicken
gehakt khuh·<u>hahkt</u>	ground meat [mincemeat]
gehaktbal khuh·<u>hahkt</u>·bahl	meatball
geit khiet	goat
geitenkaas <u>khie</u>·tuhn·kaas	goat cheese
gekonfijte vrucht khuh·kohn·<u>fie</u>·tuh fruhkht	candied fruit
gekookt eitje khuh·<u>koakt</u> ie·tyuh	boiled egg
gekookte aardappel	boiled potato
khuh·<u>koak</u>·tuh <u>aar</u>·dah·puhl	
gele spercieboon <u>khay</u>·luh <u>spehr</u>·see·boan	butter bean
gember <u>khehm</u>·buhr	ginger
gemengde grill khuh·<u>mehng</u>·duh khrihl	mixed grill
gemengde groenten	mixed vegetables
khuh·<u>mehng</u>·duh khroon·tuhn	
gemengde kruiden	mixed herbs
khuh·<u>mehng</u>·duh <u>kraw</u>·duhn	
gemengde noten khuh·<u>mehng</u>·duh <u>noa</u>·tuhn	assorted nuts
gemengde salade	mixed salad
khuh·<u>mehng</u>·duh saa·<u>laa</u>·duh	
gerookte paling khuh·<u>roak</u>·tuh <u>paa</u>·lihng	smoked eel
gerookte zalm khuh·<u>roak</u>·tuh zahlm	smoked salmon
geroosterd brood khuh·<u>roas</u>·tuhrt broat	toast
geroosterde aardappel	roast potato
khuh·<u>roas</u>·tuhr·duh <u>aar</u>·dah·puhl	
geroosterde kip khuh·<u>roas</u>·tuhr·duh kihp	roast chicken
gestoofd fruit khuh·<u>stoaft</u> frawt	stewed fruit
gestoomde vis khuh·<u>stoam</u>·duh fihs	steamed fish
getapt bier khuh·<u>tahpt</u> beer	draft [draught] beer
gevogelte khuh·<u>foa</u>·khuhl·tuh	fowl
gevulde olijf khuh·<u>fuhl</u>·duh oa·<u>lief</u>	stuffed olive
gezouten pinda khuh·<u>zow</u>·tuhn <u>pihn</u>·dah	salted peanut

gin-tonic _zhihn·toh·nihk_	gin and tonic
goulash _khoo·lahsh_	goulash
grapefruit _krayp·froot_	grapefruit
granaatappel _khraa·naat·ah·puhl_	pomegranate
griesmeelpudding _khrees·mayl·puh·dihng_	semolina pudding
groene erwt _khroo·nuh ehrt_	green pea
groene paprika _khroo·nuh paa·pree·kaa_	green pepper
groene salade _khroo·nuh saa·laa·duh_	green salad
groentebouillon _khroon·tuh·boo·yohn_	vegetable broth
groente _khroon·tuh_	vegetable
groentesoep _khroon·tuh·soop_	vegetable soup
Goudse kaas _khowt·suh kaas_	Gouda cheese
guave _kwaa·fuh_	guava
Haagse bluf _haakh·suh bluhf_	dessert of whipped egg white with red currant sauce
haas _haas_	hare
hachee _hah·shay_	meat stew
hamlap _hahm·lahp_	pork steak
hapje _hahp·yuh_	snack
hapjes vooraf _hahp·yuhs foar·ahf_	appetizers
hardgekookt _hahrt·khuh·koakt_	hard-boiled (egg)
harder _hahr·duhr_	gray mullet
haring _haa·rihng_	herring
haringsalade _haa·rihng·saa·laa·duh_	salad of salted or marinated herring
havermoutpap _haa·fuhr·mowt·pahp_	porridge
hazelnoten _haa·zuhl·noa·tuhn_	hazelnuts
heek _hayk_	hake
heet water _hayt vaa·tuhr_	hot water
heilbot _hiel·boht_	halibut
heldere soep _hehl·duh·ruh soop_	broth

hete bliksem _hay•tuh blihk•suhm_	dish of potatoes, bacon & apple
hete pepersaus _hay•tuh pay•purh•sows_	hot pepper sauce
Hollandse biefstuk _hoh•lahnt•suh beef•stuhk_	Dutch steak
honing _hoa•nihng_	honey
hoorntje _hoarn•tyuh_	cream horn (dessert)
hopjes _hohp•yuhs_	coffee-flavored toffee
huiswijn _haws•vien_	house wine
hutspot _huhts•poht_	stew made of mashed potatoes with carrots and onions or with curly kale
hutspot met klapstuk _huhts•poht meht klahp•stuhk_	mashed potatoes, carrots and onions served with rib of beef
huzarensalade _hew•zaa•ruhn•saa•laa•duh_	mixture of potato, raw vegetables and meat with mayonnaise
ijs _ies_	ice
in beslag gebakken _ihn buh•slahkh khuh•bah•kuhn_	fried in batter
in de pan gebakken vis _ihn duh pahn khuh•bah•kuhn fihs_	fried fish
in knoflook _ihn knohf•loak_	in garlic
in olie _ihn oa•lee_	in oil
in de oven gebakken vis _ihn duh oa•fuhn khuh•bah•kuhn fihs_	baked fish
inktvis _ihnkt•fihs_	squid
inwendige organen _ihn•wehn•dih•khuh ohr•khaa•nuhn_	giblets
jachtschotel _yahkht•skhoa•tuhl_	meat casserole with potatoes
jam _zhehm_	jam
jenever _yuh•nay•vuhr_	gin

jeneverbes *yuh·nay·vuhr·behs*	juniper berry
jong geitenvlees *yohng khie·tuhn·flays*	young goat
jonge eend *yohng·uh aynt*	duckling
jus *zhew*	gravy
kaas *kaas*	cheese
kaasplank *kaas·plahnk*	cheese board
kabeljauw *kaa·buhl·yow*	cod
kalfskarbonade *kahlfs·kahr·boa·naa·duh*	veal chop
kalfsoester *kahlfs·oos·tuhr*	veal escalope
kalfsvlees *kahlfs·flays*	*veal*
kalfszwezerik *kahlfs·zvay·zuh·rihk*	sweetbread
kalkoen *kahl·koon*	turkey
kammossel *kahm·moh·suhl*	scallop
kaneel *kaa·nayl*	cinnamon
kappertje *kah·puhr·tyuh*	caper
karbonade *karh·boa·naa·duh*	chop
karnemelk *kahr·nuh·mehlk*	buttermilk
karwij *kahr·wie*	caraway
kastanje *kahs·tahn·yus*	chestnut
katenspek *kaa·tuhn·spehk*	smoked bacon
kaviaar *kaa·vee·yaar*	caviar
kers *kehrs*	cherry
kerstomaat *kehrs·toa·maat*	cherry tomato
kervel *kehr·fuhl*	chervil
kidneyboon *kiht·nee·boan*	kidney bean
kikkererwt *kih·kuhr·ehrt*	chickpea
kip *kihp*	chicken
kippenborst *kih·puhn·bohrst*	breast of chicken
kippenlever *kih·puhn·lay·fuhr*	chicken liver
kippensoep *kih·puhn·soop*	chicken soup
kiwi *kee·vee*	kiwi

klapstuk _klahp_·stuhk	beef rib
kluif _klawf_	pig's knuckle
knakworst _knahk_·vohrst	wiener
knoedel _knoo_·duhl	dumpling
knoflook _knohf_·loak	garlic
knoflook mayonaise	garlic mayonnaise
knohf·loak·maa·yoh·_neh_·suh	
knoflooksaus _knohf_·loak·sows	garlic sauce
knolselderij _knohl_·sehl·duh·rie	celery [celeriac]
koekje _kook_·yuh	cookie [biscuit]
koffie _kohf_·fee	coffee
kokos _koa_·kohs	coconut
kokosmakroon _koa_·kohs·maa·kroan	coconut macaroon
komijn koa·_mien_	cumin
komijnekaas koa·_mie_·nuh·kaas	cheese with cumin seeds
komkommer kohm·_kohm_·muhr	cucumber
komkommersalade	
kohm·_kohm_·muhr·saa·_laa_·duh	cucumber salad
konijn koa·_nien_	rabbit
koninginnensoep _koa_·nihng·_ihn_·uhn·soop	cream of chicken
kool _koal_	cabbage
koolrabi _koal_·raa·bee	kohlrabi
koolsla _koal_·slaa	coleslaw
koolzuurhoudend (water)	
koal·zewr·_how_·duhnt (_vaa_·tuhr)	sparkling (water)
koolzuurvrij (water) _koal_·zewr·frie (_vaa_·tuhr)	still (water)
koriander koh·ree·_ahn_·duhr	cilantro [coriander]
korstdeeg _kohrst_·daykh	puff pastry
kort gebakken kohrt khuh·_bah_·kuhn	rare
kotelet koa·tuh·_leht_	chop, cutlet
krab krap	crab

kreeft *krayft*		lobster
krentenbol *krehn·tuhn·bohl*		currant bun
krentenbrood *krehn·tuhn·broat*		currant bread
kroepoek *kroo·pook*		shrimp [prawn] crackers
kroket *kroa·keht*		croquettes
kropsla *krohp·slaa*		cabbage lettuce
kruiden *kraw·duhn*		herbs
kruidnagel *krawt·naa·khuhl*		clove
kruisbes *kraws·behs*		gooseberry
kwarktaart *kvahrk·taart*		light cheesecake
kwartelvlees *kvahr·tuhl·flays*		quail
kweegelei *kvay·zhuh·lei*		quince jelly
kwets *kvehts*		blue plum
lamsbout *lahms·bowt*		leg of lamb
lamsstoofschotel *lahms·stoaf·skhoa·tuhl*		lamb stew
lamsvlees *lahms·flays*		lamb
lamszadel *lahms·zaa·duhl*		saddle (lamb)
laurierblad *low·reer·blaht*		bay leaf
lekkerbekje *leh·kuhr·behk·yuh*		breaded fillet of haddock
lendebiefstuk *lehn·duh·beef·stuhk*		fillet, rump steak
lendevlees *lehn·duh·flays*		loin meat
lente-uitje *lehn·tuh·aw·tyuh*		spring onion
lever *lay·fuhr*		liver
likeur *lee·kur*		liqueur
limoen *lee·moon*		lime
limoensap *lee·moon·sahp*		lime juice
limonade *lee·moa·naa·duh*		lemonade
limonadesiroop *lee·moa·naa·duh·see·roap*		fruit drink concentrate of various flavors
linze *lihn·zuh*		lentil
loempia *loom·pee·yaa*		spring roll

lofsalade _lohf·sah·laa·duh_ — salad of raw chicory rings

lopend buffet _loa·puhnt bew·feht_ — buffet

maïs _mah·ees_ — sweet corn

makreel _maa·krayl_ — mackerel

mandarijn _mahn·daa·rien_ — tangerine

marmelade _mahr·muh·laa·duh_ — marmalade

marsepein _mahr·suh·pien_ — marzipan

mayonaise _maa·yoh·neh·suh_ — mayonnaise

melk _mehlk_ — milk

meloen _muh·loon_ — melon

metworst _meht·vohrst_ — spicy sausage

mie _mee_ — noodles

mierikswortel _mee·rihks·wohr·tuhl_ — horseradish

milkshake _mihlk·shayk_ — milk shake

mineraalwater _mee·nuh·raal·vaa·tuhr_ — mineral water

moerbei _moor·bie_ — mulberry

moorkop _mohr·kohp_ — chocolate éclair

mossel _moh·suhl_ — mussel

mosterd _mohs·tuhrt_ — mustard

mousserende wijn _moo·say·ruhn·duh vien_ — sparkling wine

mul _muhl_ — red mullet

munt _muhnt_ — mint

muntthee _muhnt·tay_ — mint tea

nasi goreng _naa·see khoa·rehng_ — Indonesian fried rice with spices, meat and egg

nectarine _nehk·taa·ree·nuh_ — nectarine

niertjes _neer·tyuhs_ — kidneys

nieuwe haring _neeew·vuh haa·rihng_ — freshly caught, salt-cured herring

noga _noa·gaa_ — nougat

nootmuskaat _noat·muhs·kaat_ — nutmeg

octopus <u>ohk</u>·toa·puhs	octopus
oester <u>oos</u>·tuhr	oyster
oesterzwam <u>oos</u>·tuhr·zwahm	oyster mushroom
olie en azijn <u>oa</u>·lee ehn aa·<u>zien</u>	oil and vinegar
olijf oa·<u>lief</u>	olive
omelet <u>oh</u>·muh·leht	omelet
ossenhaas <u>oh</u>·suhn·haas	tenderloin (beef)
ossenstaartsoep <u>oh</u>·suhn·staart·<u>soop</u>	oxtail soup
oude kaas <u>ow</u>·duh kaas	hard cheese
paddenstoel <u>pah</u>·duhn·stool	field mushroom
paling <u>paa</u>·lihng	eel
pannenkoek pah·<u>nuhn</u>·kook	pancake
paprika <u>paa</u>·pree·kaa	(sweet) pepper
parelhoen <u>paa</u>·ruhl·hoon	guinea fowl
passievrucht <u>pah</u>·see·fruhkht	passion fruit
pasta <u>pahs</u>·taa	pasta
pastei pahs·<u>tie</u>	pie
pasteideeg pahs·<u>tie</u>·daykh	pastry
pasteitje (vol-au-vent) pahs·<u>tie</u>·tyuh (<u>fohl</u>·oa·fahn)	pastry filled with meat or fish
pastinaak pahs·tee·<u>naak</u>	parsnips
patat paa·<u>taht</u>	French fries [chips]
paté paa·<u>tay</u>	paté
patrijs paa·<u>tries</u>	partridge
peer payr	pear
pekelvlees <u>pay</u>·kuhl·flays	sliced, salted meat
pens pehns	tripe
peper <u>pay</u>·puhr	black pepper
pepernoten <u>pay</u>·puhr·noa·tuhn	gingerbread nuts
perzik pehr·zihk	peach
peterselie <u>pay</u>·tuhr·say·lee	parsley

peultjes *pul·tyuhs*	sugar peas
piepkuiken *peep·kaw·kuhn*	spring chicken
pikant *pee·kahnt*	hot (spicy)
pikant worstje *pee·kahnt vohrst·yuh*	spicy sausage
pils *pihls*	lager
pinda *pihn·daa*	peanut
pindasaus *pihn·daa·sows*	peanut sauce
pitabroodje *pee·taa·broat·yuh*	pita bread
plaatselijke specialiteit *plaats·uh·luh·kuh spay·shaa·lee·tiet*	local speciality
poffertje *poh·fuhr·tyuh*	tiny pancake
pompoen *pohm·poon*	pumpkin
portie *pohr·see*	portion
prei *prie*	leek
prinsessenboon *prihn·seh·suhn·boan*	haricot bean
pruim *prawm*	plum
raap *raap*	turnip
rabarber *raa·bahr·buhr*	rhubarb
radijs *raa·dies*	radish
rammenas *rah·muh·nahs*	winter radish
rauw *row*	raw
reebout *ray·bowt*	venison
ribstuk *rihp·stuhk*	rib
rijst *riest*	rice
rijstebrij *ries·tuh·brie*	rice pudding
risotto *ree·soh·toa*	risotto
rivierkreeft *ree·feer·krayft*	crayfish
rode kool *roa·duh koal*	red cabbage
rode paprika *roa·duh paa·pree·kaa*	sweet red pepper
rode peper *roa·duh pay·puhr*	chili pepper
roerei *roor·ie*	scrambled egg

rog *rohkh*	ray
roggebrood <u>roh</u>·khuh·broat	rye bread
rollade roh·<u>laa</u>·duh	meat roll
romig <u>roa</u>·mihkh	creamy
rookvlees <u>roak</u>·flays	smoked or smoke-dried beef
room roam	cream
roomijs <u>roam</u>·ies	ice cream
roomsoep <u>roam</u>·soop	cream soup
rosbief <u>rohs</u>·beef	roast beef
rozemarijn <u>roa</u>·zuh·maa·<u>rijn</u>	rosemary
rozijn roa·<u>zien</u>	raisin
rum ruhm	rum
rundvlees <u>ruhnt</u>·flays	beef
Russisch ei <u>ruh</u>·sees <u>ie</u>	hard-boiled egg filled with mayonnaise, garnished with fish and salad
saffraan sah·<u>fraan</u>	saffron
sajur lodeh <u>saa</u>·yoor <u>loa</u>·deh	Indonesian vegetable dish
salade saa·<u>laa</u>·duh	salad
salie <u>saa</u>·lee	sage
sandwich <u>sehnt</u>·wihtsh	sandwich
sap sahp	juice
sardientje sahr·<u>deen</u>·tyuh	sardine
saté saa·<u>tay</u>	meat on skewers
saucijzenbroodje sow·<u>sie</u>·zuhn·<u>broat</u>·yuh	sausage roll
saucijs sow·<u>sies</u>	sausage
saus sows	sauce
savooiekool saa·<u>voa</u>·yuh·koal	savoy cabbage
schaaldieren <u>skhaal</u>·dee·ruhn	shellfish
schapenkaas <u>skhaa</u>·puhn·kaas	ewe's milk cheese
schapenvlees <u>skhaa</u>·puhn·flays	mutton

schelpdier _skhehlp_·deer	shellfish, clam
schelvis _skhehl_·fihs	haddock
schenkel _skhehn_·kuhl	shank (top of leg)
schimmelkaas _skhih_·muhl·kaas	blue cheese
schnitzel _shniht_·zuhl	veal or pork cutlet
schol skhohl	plaice
schuimgebakje _skhawm_·khuh·bahk·yuh	meringue
selderij _sehl_·duh·rie	celery
sinaasappel _see_·naas·ah·puhl	orange
sinaasappelsap _see_·naas·ah·puhl·sahp	orange juice
siroop see·_roap_	syrup
sjalotten shaa·_loh_·tuhn	shallots
sla slaa	lettuce
slagroom _slakh_·roam	sweet whipped cream
slak _slahk_	snail
slasaus _slaa_·sows	salad dressing
snijbonen _snie_·boa·nuhn	sliced green beans
snoepje _snoop_·yuh	candy [sweet]
soep soop	soup
soesje _soos_·yuh	pastry filled with whipped cream
specerijen spay·suh·_rie_·yuhn	spices
specialiteiten van de chef-kok _spay_·shaa·lee·_tie_·tuhn fahn duh _shehf_·kohk	specialities of the house
speculaas spay·kew·laas	spiced cookie [biscuit]
speenvarken _spayn_·fahr·kuhn	suckling pig
spek spehk	bacon
spekpannenkoek _spehk_·pah·nuhn·kook	bacon pancake
sperzieboon _spehr_·see·boan	green bean
spiegelei _spee_·khuhl·ie	fried egg
spijkerrog _spie_·kuhr·rohkh	skate (fish)

spinazie *spee·naa·zee* — spinach
spitskool *spihts·koal* — type of cabbage
sprits *sprihts* — Dutch shortbread
sprot *sproht* — sprat (fish)
spruitje *spraw·tyuh* — Brussel sprout
stamppot *stahm·poht* — one-pan dish with vegetables and mashed potatoes

sterk *stehrk* — strong (flavor)
stervrucht *stehr·fruhkht* — star fruit
stokbrood *stohk·broat* — French-style bread
stokvisschotel *stohk·fihs·skhoa·tuhl* — oven stew of dried cod
stoofschotel *stoaf·skhoa·tuhl* — casserole, stew
stroop *stroap* — molasses
stroopwafel *stroap·vaa·fuhl* — two waffles with syrup in between them

suiker *saw·kuhr* — sugar
suikerglazuur *saw·kuhr·khlaa·zewr* — icing
sultanarozijn *suhl·taa·naa·roa·zien* — sultana raisin
taart *taart* — tart
taartje *taart·yuh* — tartlette
tafelwijn *taa·fuhl·vien* — table wine
tafelzuur *taa·fuhl·zewr* — pickle
tahoe/tofoe *taa·hoo/toa·few* — tofu
tarbot *tahr·boa* — turbot
tartaartje *tahr·taar·tyuh* — ground steak
taugé *tow·gay* — bean sprouts
thee *tay* — tea
tijm *tiem* — thyme
toast *toast* — toast
toeristenmenu *too·rihs·tuhn·muh·new* — tourist menu
tomaat *toa·maat* — tomato

tomatenketchup *toa·maa·tuhn·keht·shuhp*	ketchup
tomatensaus *toa·maa·tuhn·sows*	tomato sauce
tomatensoep *toa·maa·tuhn·soop*	tomato soup
tompoes *tohm·poos*	cake slice with custard filling
tong *tohng*	tongue, sole
tonic *toh·nihk*	tonic water
tonijn *toa·nien*	tuna
tosti *tohs·tee*	toasted sandwich
tournedos *toor·nay·dohs*	fillet steak
truffel *truh·fuhl*	truffle
tuinboon *tawn·boan*	broad bean
tuinkers *tawn·kehrs*	cress
tulband *tuhl·bahnd*	turban-shaped fruit cake
ui *aw*	onion
uiensoep *aw·yuhn·soop*	onion soup
uitsmijter *awt·smie·tuhr*	snack of bread, ham and fried eggs
vanille *vaa·nee·yuh*	vanilla
varkenshaas *fahr·kuhns·haas*	tenderloin (pork)
varkenskotelet *fahr·kuhns·koa·tuh·leht*	pork chop
varkenspootjes *fahr·kuhns·poat·yuhs*	pigs' feet
varkensvlees *fahr·kuhns·flays*	pork
varkensworstje *fahr·kuhns·vohrst·yuh*	pork sausage
veenbes *fayn·behs*	cranberry
venkel *fehn·kuhl*	fennel
vermicellisoep *fehr·mee·seh·lee·soop*	clear noodle soup
vermout *fuhr·mowt*	vermouth
vers fruit *fehrs frawt*	fresh fruit
verse kwark *fehr·suh kvahrk*	fresh-curd cheese
vijg *fiekh*	fig
vinaigrette *fih·nuh·kreht*	vinaigrette

vis *fihs*	fish
vispastei *fihs·pahs·tie*	chopped fish in a pastry shell
vissoep *fihs·soop*	fish soup
visstick *fihs·stihk*	fish stick
vla *flaa*	custard
vlees *flays*	meat (general)
vleesbouillon *flays·boo·yohn*	meat broth
vleespastei *flays·pahs·tie*	chopped meat in a pastry shell
volkorenmeel *fohl·koa·ruhn·mayl*	wholewheat flour
voorn *foarn*	rock-bass (fish)
vruchtendrank *fruhkh·tuhn·drahngk*	fruit drink
vruchtensap *fruhkh·tuhn·sahp*	fruit juice
vruchtenvlaai *fruhkh·tuhn·flaai*	Limburg fruit flan
wafel *vaa·fuhl*	waffle
walnoot *vahl·noat*	walnut
warme chocolademelk *vahr·muh shoa·koa·laa·duh·mehlk*	hot chocolate
waterkastanje *vaa·tuhr·kahs·tahn·yuh*	water chestnut
waterkers *vaa·tuhr·kehrs*	watercress
watermeloen *vaa·tuhr·muh·loon*	watermelon
wentelteefje *vehn·tuhl·tayf·yuh*	French toast
wienerschnitzel *vee·nuhr shniht·suhl*	breaded veal slices
wijn *vien*	wine
wijting *vie·tihng*	whiting
wild *vihlt*	game
wild zwijn *vihlt zvien*	wild boar
wilde eend *vihl·duh aynt*	wild duck
witlof *viht·lohf*	chicory
witlofsalade *viht·lohf·saa·laa·duh*	chicory salad
witte asperge (met saus) *vih·tuh ah·spehr·zhuh (meht sows)*	white asparagus (with sauce)

witte bonen <u>vih</u>•tuh <u>boa</u>•nuhn	haricot beans
witte druif <u>vih</u>•tuh	drawf green grape
witte kool <u>vih</u>•tuh koal	white cabbage
witte saus <u>vih</u>•tuh sows	white sauce
wodka <u>vohd</u>•kaa	vodka
worstje <u>vohrst</u>•yuh	sausage
wortel <u>vohr</u>•tuhls	carrot
wortelsalade <u>vohr</u>•tuhl•saa•<u>laa</u>•duh	raw grated carrot
yoghurt <u>yoh</u>•khuhrt	yogurt
zacht gekookt zahkht khuh•<u>koakt</u>	soft-boiled
zachte kaas <u>zahkh</u>•tuh kaas	soft cheese
zalm zahlm	salmon
zandgebak <u>zahnd</u>•khuh•bahk	shortbread, shortcake
zeebaars <u>zay</u>•baars	sea bass
zeebliek <u>zay</u>•bleek	whitebait
zeebrasem <u>zay</u>•braa•suhm	sea bream
zeeduivel <u>zay</u>•daw•fuhl	monkfish
zeekat <u>zay</u>•kaht	cuttlefish
zeepaling <u>zay</u>•paa•lihng	conger eel
zoetzure saus <u>zoot</u>•zew•ruh sows	sweet and sour sauce
zoetje <u>zoot</u>•yuh	sweetener
zoetwatervis zoot•<u>vaa</u>•tuhr•fihs	freshwater fish
zout zowt	salt
zoutwatervis zowt•<u>vaa</u>•tuhr•fihs	saltwater fish
zure bom <u>zew</u>•ruh bohm	large gherkin
zure haring <u>zew</u>•ruh <u>haa</u>•rihng	pickled herring [rollmops]
zuring <u>zew</u>•rihng	sorrel
zuurkool <u>zewr</u>•koal	sauerkraut
zwaardvis <u>zvaart</u>•fihs	swordfish
zwarte bes <u>zvahr</u>•tuh behs	blackcurrant

People

Conversation

ESSENTIAL

Hello./Hi!	**Dag./Hallo!** dakh/hah·<u>loa</u>
How are you?	**Hoe gaat het met u?** hoo khaat heht meht ew
Fine, thanks.	**Prima, dank u.** <u>pree</u>·maa dangk ew
Excuse me!	**Meneer/Mevrouw!** muh·<u>nayr</u>/muh·<u>frow</u>
(to a man/woman)	
Do you speak English?	**Spreekt u Engels?** spraykt ew <u>ehng</u>·uhls
What's your name?	**Hoe heet u?** hoo hayt ew
My name is...	**Mijn naam is...** mien naam ihs...
Nice to meet you.	**Aangenaam.** <u>aan</u>·khuh·naam
Where are you from?	**Waar komt u vandaan?** vaar kohmt ew fahn·<u>daan</u>
I'm from the	**Ik kom uit de Verenigde Staten/Groot-Brittannië.**
U.S./U.K.	ihk kohm awt duh fuhr·<u>ay</u>·nihkh·duh <u>staa</u>·tuhn/
	<u>khroat</u>·brih·<u>tah</u>·nee·yuh
What do you do?	**Wat doet u in het dagelijks leven?**
	vaht doot ew ihn heht <u>daa</u>·khuh·luks <u>lay</u>·fuhn
I work for...	**Ik werk bij...** ihk vehrk bie...
I'm a student.	**Ik ben student.** ihk behn stew·<u>dehnt</u>
I'm retired.	**Ik ben met pensioen.** ihk behn meht pehn·shoon
Do you like...?	**Houdt u van...?** howt ew fahn...
Goodbye.	**Dag.** dakh
See you later.	**Tot ziens.** toht zeens

Language Difficulties

Do you speak English?	**Spreekt u Engels?**	*spraykt ew ehng·uhls*
Does anyone here speak English?	**Is er hier iemand die Engels spreekt?** *ihs ehr heer ee·mahnt dee ehng·uhls spraykt*	
I don't speak Dutch.	**Ik spreek geen Nederlands.** *ihk sprayk khayn nay·duhr·lahnts*	
I don't speak much Dutch.	**Ik spreek maar weinig Nederlands.** *ihk sprayk maar vie·nihkh nay·duhr·lahnts*	
Can you speak more slowly?	**Kunt u iets langzamer spreken?** *kuhnt ew eets lahng·zaa·muhr spray·kuhn*	
Can you repeat that?	**Kunt u dat herhalen?** *kuhnt ew daht hehr·haa·luhn*	
Excuse me?	**Pardon?** *pahr·dohn*	
What was that?	**Wat zegt u?** *vaht zehkht ew*	
Can you spell it?	**Kunt u dat spellen?** *kuhnt ew daht spehl·ehn*	
Can you write it down?	**Kunt u het opschrijven?** *kuhnt ew heht ohp·skhrie·fuhn*	
Can you translate this for me?	**Kunt u dit voor mij vertalen?** *kuhnt ew diht foar mie fuhr·taa·luhn*	
What does this mean?	**Wat betekent dit?** *vaht buh·tay·kuhnt diht*	
I (don't) understand.	**Ik begrijp het (niet).** *ihk buh·khrayp heht (neet)*	
Do you understand?	**Begrijpt u het?** *buh·khraypt ew heht*	

YOU MAY HEAR…

Ik spreek slechts weinig Engels. *ihk sprayk slehkhts vie·nihkh ehng·uhls*	I only speak a little English.
Ik spreek geen Engels. *ihk sprayk khayn ehng·uhls*	I don't speak English.

When addressing people you don't know, use **u** (formal you) or **meneer** (sir) and **mevrouw** (ma'am or madam), particularly with strangers and older people. It is impolite to address someone with the familiar **jij** and **je** (**jullie**, in the plural) until invited to do so.

Making Friends

Hello./Hi!	**Dag./Hallo!** *dakh/hah·loa*
Good morning.	**Goedemorgen.** *khoo·duh·mohr·khuhn*
Good afternoon.	**Goedemiddag.** *khoo·duh·mih·dahkh*
Good evening.	**Goedenavond.** *khoo·duh·naa·fohnt*
My name is...	**Mijn naam is...** *mien naam ihs...*
What's your name?	**Hoe heet u?** *hoo hayt ew*
I'd like to introduce you to...	**Ik wil u graag voorstellen aan...** *ihk vihl ew khraakh foar·steh·luhn aan...*
Nice to meet you.	**Aangenaam.** *aan·khuh·naam*
How are you?	**Hoe gaat het met u?** *hoo khaat heht meht ew*
Fine, thanks.	**Prima, dank u.** *pree·ma dangk ew*
And you?	**En met u?** *en meht ew*

In the Netherlands, upon meeting, it is customary to shake hands and to use a greeting appropriate for the time of day. Close friends may kiss cheeks (left, right, left) and say **Hoe gaat het?** (How are you?) or **Alles goed?** (Is everything alright?). You'll find surnames are used more frequently than first names, even when answering the phone. When entering a store, greet the shop attendant by saying **goedemorgen, goedemiddag,** or **goedenavond** (good morning, good afternoon, good evening). When leaving you can say **dag** or **tot ziens** (goodbye or see you soon).

Travel Talk

I'm here...	**Ik ben hier...** *ihk behn heer...*
on business	**voor zaken** *foar zaa·kuhn*
on vacation [holiday]	**met vakantie** *meht faa·kahn·see*
studying	**voor studie** *foar stew·dee*
I'm staying for...	**Ik blijf...** *ihk blief...*
I've been here...	**Ik ben hier al...** *ihk behn heer ahl...*
a day	**een dag** *uhn dahkh*
a week	**een week** *uhn vayk*

a month	**een maand** _uhn maant_
Where are you from?	**Waar komt u vandaan?**
	vaar kohmt ew fahn·daan
I'm from...	**Ik kom uit...** _ihk kohm awt..._

For Numbers, see page 165.

Personal

Who are you with?	**Met wie bent u?** _meht vee behnt ew_
I'm on my own.	**Ik ben in mijn eentje.** _ihk behn ihn mien ayn·tyuh_
I'm with...	**Ik ben met...** _ihk behn meht..._
my husband/wife	**mijn man/vrouw** _mien mahn/frow_
my boyfriend/ girlfriend	**mijn vriend/vriendin** _mien freent/freen·dihn_
a friend	**een vriend** _uhn freent_
a colleague	**een collega** _uhn koh·lay·khaa_
When's your birthday?	**Wanneer bent u jarig?** _vah·nayr behnt ew yaa·rikh_
How old are you?	**Hoe oud bent u?** _hoo owt behnt ew_
I'm...	**Ik ben...** _ihk behn..._
Are you married?	**Bent u getrouwd?** _behnt ew khuh·trowt_
I'm...	**Ik ben...** _ihk behn..._
single/in a relationship	**ongetrouwd/in een relatie** _ohn·khuh·trowt/ihn uhn ray·laa·tsee_
engaged	**verloofd** _fehr·loaft_
married	**getrouwd** _khuh·trowt_
divorced	**gescheiden** _khuh·skhie·duhn_
separated	**uit elkaar** _awt ehl·kaar_
I'm in a relationship.	**Ik heb een relatie.** _ihk hehp uhn ray·laat·see_
I'm widowed.	**Ik ben weduwnaar** _m_/**weduwe** _f_
	ihk behn vay·dew·naar/vay·dew·uh
Do you have children/ grandchildren?	**Heeft u kinderen/kleinkinderen?**
	hayft ew kihn·duh·ruhn/klien·kihn·duh·ruhn

Work & School

What do you do?	**Wat doet u in het dagelijks leven?**
	vaht doot ew ihn heht daa•khuh•luks lay•fuhn
What are you studying?	**Wat studeert u?** *vaht stew•dayrt ew*
I'm studying...	**Ik studeer...** *ihk stew•dayr...*
I...	**ik...** *ihk*
work full-/part-time	**werk voltijds/deeltijds** *wehrk fohl•tiets/dayl•tiets*
am unemployed	**ben werkeloos** *behn wehr•keh•loas*
work at home	**ben thuiswerker** *behn taws•wehr•kehr*
Who do you work for?	**Voor wie werkt u?** *foar vee vehrkt ew*
I work for...	**Ik werk voor...** *ihk vehrk foar...*
Here's my business card.	**Hier is mijn visitekaartje.**
	heer ihs mien fee•zee•tuh•kaart•yuh

For Business Travel, see page 141.

Weather

What's the weather forecast?	**Wat is het weerbericht?**
	vaht ihs heht vayr•buh•rihkht
What beautiful/ terrible weather!	**Wat een mooi/vreselijk weer!**
	vaht uhn moay/fray•suh•luhk vayr
It's cool/warm.	**Het is koel/warm.** *heht ihs kool/vahrm*
It's hot/cold.	**Het is heet/koud.** *heht ihs hayt/kowt*
It's rainy/sunny.	**Het is regenachtig/zonnig.**
	heht ihs ray•khuhn•ahkh•tikh/zoh•nihkh
It's snowy/icy.	**Het sneeuwt/vriest.** *heht snaywt/freest*
Do I need a jacket/ an umbrella?	**Moet ik een jas/paraplu meenemen?**
	moot ihk uhn jahs/paa•raa•plew may•nay•muhn

For Temperature, see page 170.

ESSENTIAL

Would you like to go out for a drink/meal?	**Heb je zin om iets te gaan drinken/uit eten te gaan?** *hehp yuh zihn ohm eets tuh gaan drihn•kuhn/awt ay•tuhn tuh gaan*
What are your plans for tonight/tomorrow?	**Wat zijn je plannen voor vanavond/morgen?** *vaht zien yuh plah•nuhn foar fah•naa•fohnt/mohr•khuhn*
Can I have your phone number?	**Mag ik je telefoonnummer?** *mahkh ihk yuh tay•luh•foan•nuh•muhr*
Can I join you?	**Mag ik bij je komen zitten?** *mahkh ihk bie yuh koa•muhn zih•tuhn*
Can I buy you a drink?	**Wil je iets van me drinken?** *vihl yuh eets fahn muh drihng•kuhn*
I like you.	**Ik mag je graag.** *ihk mahkh yuh khraakh*
I love you.	**Ik hou van je.** *ihk how fahn yuhft.*

The Dating Game

Would you like to go out for coffee?	**Wil je ergens koffie gaan drinken?** *vihl yuh ehr•khuhns koh•fee khaan drihng•kuhn*
Would you like to go out…?	**Zou je samen iets willen…?** *sow yeh saa•mehn eets vih•lehn khaan…*
for a drink	**drinken** *drihnk•ehn*
to dinner	**eten** *ay•tehn*
What are your plans for…?	**Wat zijn je plannen voor…?** *vaht zien yuh plah•nuhn foar…*
today	**vandaag** *fahn•daakh*
tonight	**vanavond** *fah•naa•fohnt*
tomorrow	**morgen** *mohr•khuhn*
this weekend	**dit weekend** *diht vee•kehnt*

Where would you like to go?	**Waar wil je naartoe?** *vaar vihl yuh naar too*
I'd like to go to...	**Ik wil graag naar...** *ihk vihl khraakh naar...*
Do you like...?	**Hou je van...?** *how yuh fahn...*
Can I have your number/e-mail?	**Mag ik je nummer/e-mailadres?** *mahkh ihk yuh nuh•muhr/ee•mayl•aa•drehs*
Are you on Facebook/Twitter?	**Zit je op Facebook/Twitter?** *siht yuh ohp Facebook/Twitter*
Can I join you?	**Mag ik bij je komen zitten?** *mahkh ihk bie yuh koa•muhn zih•tuhn*
You're very attractive.	**Je ziet er fantastisch uit.** *yuh zeet ehr fahn•tahs•tees awt*
Shall we go somewhere quieter?	**Zullen we een rustig plekje opzoeken?** *zuh•luhn vuh uhn ruhs•tikh plehk•yuh ohp•zoo•kuhn*

Throughout this section, the informal you is applied in Dutch.

For Communications, see page 49.

Accepting & Rejecting

| Thank you. | **Dank je. Dat zou erg leuk zijn.** |
| I'd love to. | *dangk yuh daht zow ehrkh luk zien* |

Where should we meet?	**Waar zullen we elkaar ontmoeten?**
	vaar zuh•luhn vuh ehl•kaar ohnt•moo•tuhn
I'll meet you at the bar/your hotel.	**Laten we in de bar/jouw hotel afspreken.**
	laa•tuhn vuh ihn duh bahr/yow hoa•tehl ahf•spray•kuhn
I'll come by at…	**Ik haal je om…uur op.** *ihk haal yuh ohm…uwr ohp*
Thank you, but I'm busy.	**Dank je, maar ik heb het te druk.**
	dangk yuh maar ihk hehp heht tuh druhk
I'm not interested.	**Ik heb geen interesse.** *ihk hehp khayn*
	ihn•tuh•reh•suh ihk hehp khayn ihn•tuh•reh•suh
Leave me alone, please.	**Laat me alstublieft met rust.**
	laat muh ahls•tew•bleeft meht ruhst
Stop bothering me.	**Blijf me niet steeds lastig vallen.**
	blief muh neet stayts lahs•tihkh fah•luhn

Getting Intimate

Can I hug/kiss you?	**Mag ik je omhelzen/zoenen?**
	mahkh ihk yuh ohm•hehl•zuhn/zoo•nuhn
Yes.	**Ja.** *yaa*
No.	**Nee.** *nay*
Stop!	**Stop!** *stohp*
I love you.	**Ik houd van je.** *ihk how fahn yeh*

Sexual Preferences

Are you gay?	**Ben je homo *m* / lesbisch *f*?**
	behn yuh hoa •moa/lehs•bees
I'm…	**Ik ben…** *ihk behn…*
heterosexual	**hetero** *hay•tuh•roa*
homosexual	**homo** *hoa•moa*
bisexual	**biseksueel** *bee•sehk•sew•ayl*
Do you like men/women?	**Val jij op mannen/vrouwen?**
	fahl yie ohp mah•nehn/frow•ehn

Leisure Time

ESSENTIAL

Where's the tourist information office?	**Waar is het VVV-kantoor?**
	vaar ihs heht vay·vay·vay·kahn·toar
What are the main points of interest?	**Wat zijn de bezienswaardigheden?**
	vaht zien duh buh·zeens·waar·dihkh·hay·duhn
Do you have tours in English?	**Verzorgt u excursies in het Engels?**
	fuhr·zohrkht ew ehks·kuhr·sees ihn heht ehng·uhls
Can I have a map/ guide please?	**Mag ik een kaart/gids, alstublieft?**
	mahkh ihk uhn kaart/khihts ahls·tew·bleeft

Tourist Information

Do you have any information on…?	**Heeft u informatie over…?**
	hayft ew ihn·fohr·maat·see oa·fuhr…
Can you recommend…?	**Kunt u…aanbevelen?**
	kuhnt ew…aan·buh·fay·luhn
a boat trip	**een rondvaart** *uhn rohnt·faart*
an excursion	**een excursie** *uhn eks·kuhr·see*
a sightseeing tour	**een toeristische rondrit**
	uhn too·rihs·tee·suh rohnt·riht

VVV, Vereniging voor Vreemdelingenverkeer (tourist information offices), are located throughout the Netherlands, and offer a number of services such as assisting in travel arrangements, providing information about attractions and cultural events, booking tickets and making reservations.

On Tour

I'd like to go on the tour to…	**Ik wil graag de excursie doen naar…** *ihk vihl khraakh duh ehks•kuhr•see doon naar…*
Are there tours in English?	**Zijn er excursies in het Engels?** *zien ehr ehks•kuhr•sees ihn heht ehng•uhls*
What time do we leave/return?	**Hoe laat vertrekken we/komen we terug?** *hoo laat fuhr•treh•kuhn vuh/koa•muhn vuh truhkh*
Can we stop here…?	**Kunnen we hier stoppen…?** *kuh•nuhn vuh heer stoh•puhn…*
to take photographs	**om foto's te nemen** *ohm foa•toas tuh nay•muhn*
to buy souvenirs	**om souvenirs te kopen** *ohm soo•fuh•neers tuh koa•puhn*
to use the restrooms [toilets]	**om naar het toilet te gaan** *ohm naar heht tvaa•leht tuh khaan*
Is there access for the disabled?	**Is het toegankelijk voor gehandicapten?** *ihs heht too•khahn•kuh•luhk foar khuh•hehn•dee•kehp•tuhn*

For Tickets, see page 19.

Seeing the Sights

Where is/are…?	**Waar is/zijn…?** *vaar ihs/zien…*
the battleground	**het slagveld** *heht slahkh•fehlt*
the botanical garden	**de botanische tuin** *duh boa•taa•nee•suh tawn*
the castle	**het kasteel** *heht kahs•tayl*
the downtown area	**het stadscentrum** *heht staht•sehn•truhm*
the fountain	**de fontein** *duh fohn•tien*
the library	**de bibliotheek** *duh bee•blee•oa•tayk*
the market	**de markt** *duh mahrkt*
the museum	**het museum** *heht mew•zay•uhm*
the old town	**het oude stadsgedeelte** *heht ow•duh stahts•khuh•dayl•tuh*

the opera house	**de opera** *duh oa•peh•raa*
the palace	**het paleis** *heht paa•lies*
the park	**het park** *heht pahrk*
the ruins	**de ruïnes** *duh rew•ee•nuhs*
the shopping area	**de winkels** *duh vihn•kuhls*
the town square	**het stadsplein** *heht stahts•plien*
Can you show me on the map?	**Kunt u dat op de kaart laten zien?** *kuhnt ew daht ohp duh kaart laa•tuhn zeen*

It's…	**Het is…** *heht ihs…*
amazing	**verbazingwekkend** *fehr•baa•sihng•weh•kehnt*
beautiful	**mooi** *moay*
boring	**saai** *saay*
interesting	**interessant** *ihn•tuh•reh•sahnt*
magnificent	**schitterend** *skhih•teh•rehnt*
romantic	**romantisch** *roa•mahn•tees*
strange	**vreemd** *fraymt*
terrible	**vreselijk** *fray•suh•luhk*
ugly	**lelijk** *lay•luhk*
I like/don't like it.	**Ik vind het mooi/niet mooi.** *ihk fihnt heht moay/neet moay*

For Asking Directions, see page 34.

Religious Sites

Where's…?	**Waar is…?** *vaar ihs…*
the cathedral	**de kathedraal** *duh kah•teh•draal*
the church	**de kerk** *duh kehrk*
the mosque	**de moskee** *duh mohs•kay*
the synagogue	**de synagoge** *duh see•naa•khoa•khuh*
the temple	**de tempel** *duh tehm•puhl*
What time is mass/ the service?	**Hoe laat is de mis/dienst?** *hoo laat ihs duh mihs/deenst*

ESSENTIAL

Where is the market/ mall [shopping centre]?	**Waar is de markt/het winkelcentrum?** *vaar ihs duh mahrkt/heht vihn·kuhl·sehn·truhm*
I'm just looking.	**Ik kijk alleen.** *ihk kiek ah·layn*
Can you help me?	**Kunt u me helpen?** *kuhnt ew muh hehl·puhn*
I'm being helped.	**Ik word al geholpen.** *ihk vohrt ahl khuh·hohl·puhn*
How much?	**Hoeveel kost het?** *hoo·fayl kohst heht*
That one.	**Die daar.** *dee daar*
That's all, thanks.	**Meer niet, dank u.** *mayr neet dangk ew*
Where do I pay?	**Waar moet ik betalen?** *vaar moot ihk buh·taa·luhn*
I'll pay in cash/ by credit card.	**Ik wil graag contant/met een creditcard betalen.** *ihk vihl khraakh kohn·tahnt/meht uhn kreh·diht·kaart buh·taa·luhn*
A receipt, please.	**Een kwitantie, alstublieft.** *uhn kvee·tahn·see ahls·tew·bleeft*

Visiting the local markets is a fun and colorful experience. There are large as well as small markets throughout the Netherlands, where you can buy all types of goods: fruit and vegetables, cheese and bread, prepared foods, fabric and clothes, plants and flowers and so on. Some are open daily and others weekly; check with the tourist information office for exact schedules. In general, shops are open from Tuesday Saturday from 9:00 a.m. to 5:00 or 6:00 p.m. Most are closed on Monday morning and some are open on Sunday with shorter hours. In many large cities, Thursdays are late-night shopping days, with stores remaining open until 9:00 p.m.

At the Shops

Where is…?	**Waar is…?** *vaar ihs…*
the antiques store	**de antiekwinkel** *duh ahn·teek·vihn·kuhl*
the bakery	**de bakker** *duh bah·kuhr*
the bank	**de bank** *duh bahnk*
the bookstore	**de boekwinkel** *duh book·vihn·kuhl*
the clothing store [clothes shop]	**de kledingwinkel** *duh klay·dihng·vihn·kuhl*
the delicatessen	**de delicatessenwinkel** *duh day·lee·kaa·teh·suhn·vihn·kuhl*
the department store	**het warenhuis** *heht vaa·ruhn·haws*
the gift shop	**de cadeauwinkel** *duh kah·doa·vihn·kehl*
the health food store	**de reformwinkel** *duh ray·fohrm·vihn·kuhl*
the jeweler	**de juwelier** *duh yew·uh·leer*
the liquor store [off-licence]	**de slijter** *duh slie·tuhr*
the market	**de markt** *duh mahrkt*
the music store	**de muziekzaak** *duh mew·seek·vihn·kehl*
the pastry shop	**de banketbakker** *duh bang·keht·bah·kuhr*
the pharmacy [chemist]	**de apotheek** *duh ah·poa·tayk*

the produce [grocery] store	**de groentenboer** duh khroon·tuh·boor
the shoe store	**de schoenenwinkel** duh skhoon·uhn·vihn·kuhl
the shopping mall [centre]	**het winkelcentrum** heht vihn·kuhl·sehn·truhm
the souvenir store	**de souvenirwinkel** duh soo·vuh·neer·vihn·kuhl
the supermarket	**de supermarkt** duh sew·puhr·mahrkt
the tobacconist	**de tabakswinkel** duh taa·bahks·vihn·kuhl
the toy store	**de speelgoedwinkel** duh spayl·khoot·vihn·kuhl

Ask an Assistant

When does... open/close?	**Hoe laat gaat...open/dicht?** hoo laat khaat...oa·puhn/dihkht
Where is/are...?	**Waar is/zijn...?** vaar ihs/zien...
the cashier [cash desk]	**de kassa** duh kah·saa
the escalator	**de roltrap** duh rohl·trahp
the elevator [lift]	**de lift** duh lihft
the fitting rooms	**de paskamers** duh pahs·kaa·muhrs
the store guide [directory]	**winkelplattegrond** vihn·kuhl·plah·tuh·khrohnt
Can you help me?	**Kunt u me helpen?** kuhnt ew muh hehl·puhn
I'm just looking.	**Ik kijk alleen.** ihk kiek ah·layn
I'm being helped.	**Ik word al geholpen.** ihk vohrt ahl khuh·hohl·puhn
Do you have any...?	**Heeft u ook...?** hayft ew oak...
Can you show me...?	**Kunt u me...laten zien?** kuhnt ew muh...laa·tuhn zeen
Can you ship/wrap it?	**Kunt u het versturen/inpakken?** kuhnt ew heht fuhr·stew·ruhn/ihn·pah·kuhn
How much?	**Hoeveel kost het?** hoo·fayl kohst heht
That's all, thanks.	**Meer niet, dank u.** mayr neet dangk ew

For Clothing, see page 122. For Souvenirs, see page 128.

YOU MAY HEAR...

Kan ik u helpen? *kahn ihk ew hehl•puhn*   Can I help you?
Een ogenblik. *uhn oa•khuhn•blihk*   One moment.
Wat mag het zijn? *vaht mahkh heht zien*   What would you like?
Anders nog iets? *ahn•duhrs nohkh eets*   Anything else?

YOU MAY SEE...

OPEN/GESLOTEN	open/closed
GESLOTEN TIJDENS DE LUNCH	closed for lunch
PAKAMER	fitting room
CAISSIERE	cashier
ALLEEN CONTANT	cash only
CREDITKAARTEN WORDEN GEACCEPTEERD	credit cards accepted
WERKUREN	business hours
UITGANG	exit

Personal Preferences

I'd like something…	**Ik wil graag iets…**	*ihk vihl khraakh eets…*
cheap/expensive	**goedkoops/duurs**	*khoot·koaps/dewrs*
larger/smaller	**groters/kleiners**	*khroa·tuhrs/klie·nuhrs*
from this region	**uit deze streek**	*awt day·zuh strayk*
Around… euros.	**Ongeveer … euro.**	*Ohn·kheh·fayr … ur·roa*
Is it real?	**Is het echt?**	*ihs heht ehkht*

Can you show me this/that ? **Kunt u me dit/dat laten zien?**
kuhnt ew muh diht/daht laa·tuhn zeen

That's not quite what I want. **Dat is niet helemaal wat ik zoek.**
daht ihs neet hay·luh·maal vaht ihk zook

No, I don't like it. **Nee, ik vind het niet mooi.**
nay ihk fihnt heht neet moay

That's too expensive. **Dat is te duur.** *daht ihs tuh dewr*

I'd like to think about it. **Ik wil er nog even over nadenken.**
ihk vihl ehr nokh ay·fuhn oa·fuhr naa·dehn·kuhn

I'll take it. **Ik neem hem.** *ihk naym hehm*

Paying & Bargaining

How much?	**Hoeveel kost het?**	*hoo·fayl kohst heht*

I'll pay in cash/by credit card. **Ik wil graag contant/met een creditcard betalen.**
ihk vihl khraakh kohn·tahnt/meht uhn kreh·diht·kaart buh·taa·luhn

I'll pay by traveler's check. **Ik betaal met travellers cheque.**
ihk behtaal meht traveler's check

Can I have a receipt, please? **Mag ik een kwitantie, alstublieft?**
mahkh ihk uhn kvee·tahn·see ahls·tew·bleeft

That's too much. **Dat is te veel.** *daht ihs tuh fayl*

I'll give you… **Ik kan u…geven.** *ihk kahn ew… khay·fuhn*

I have only… euros. **Ik heb maar… euro.** *ihk hehp maar… ur·roa*

Is that your best price? **Is dat uw beste prijs?**

ihs daht ew beh•steh pries

Can you give me a discount? **Kunt u me korting geven?**

kuhnt ew muh kohr•tihng khay•fuhn

For Numbers, see page 165.

YOU MAY HEAR…

Hoe wilt u betalen? _hoo vihlt ew buh•taa•luhn_ How are you paying?

Uw creditkaart is geweigerd. Your credit card has been declined.
ew kreh•diht•kaart ihs khe•wie•khehrt

Legitimatie, alstublieft. ID please.
lay•khee•tee•maa•tsee, ahls•tuh•bleeft

Wij accepteren geen creditkaarten. We don't accept credit cards.
wie ahk•sehp•tay•rehn khayn
kreh•diht•kaartehn

Alleen contant geld, alstublieft. Cash only, please.
ah•layn kohn•tahnt khehlt ahls•tew•bleeft

Making a Complaint

I'd like…	**Ik wil graag…** *ihk vihl khraakh…*
to exchange this	**dit ruilen** *diht raw·luhn*
to return this	**dit terugbrengen** *diht truhkh·brehng·uhn*
a refund	**mijn geld terug** *mien khehlt truhkh*
to see the manager	**de manager spreken** *duh maa·naa·zhuhr spray·kuhn*

Services

Can you recommend…?	**Kunt u…aanbevelen?** *kuhnt ew…aan·buh·fay·luhn*
a barber	**een herenkapper** *uhn hay·ruhn·kah·puhr*
a dry cleaner	**een stomerij** *uhn stoa·muh·rie*
a hairdresser	**een dameskapper** *uhn daa·muhs·kah·puhr*
a laundromat	**een wasserette** *uhn vah·suh·reh·tuh*
a nail salon	**een nagelsalon** *uhn naa·khuhl·saa·lohn*
a spa	**een kuuroord** *uhn kewr·oart*
a travel agency	**een reisbureau** *uhn ries·bew·roa*
Can you…this?	**Kunt u dit…?** *kuhnt ew diht…*
alter	**vermaken** *fuhr·maa·kuhn*
dry clean	**stomen** *stoa·muhn*
mend	**verstellen** *fuhr·steh·luhn*
press	**persen** *pehr·suhn*
When will it be ready?	**Wanneer is het klaar?** *vah·nayr ihs heht klaar*

Hair & Beauty

I'd like…	**Ik wil graag…** *ihk vihl khraakh…*
an appointment for today/tomorrow	**een afspraak voor vandaag/morgen** *uhn ahf·spraak foar fahn·daakh/mohr·khuhn*
some color/ highlights	**een kleurspoeling/highlights** *uhn klur·spoo·lihng/highlights*
my hair styled/ blow-dried	**m'n haar laten stylen/föhnen** *muhn haar laa·tuhn stie·luhn/fuh·nuhn*

a haircut	**geknipt worden** *khuh‑knihpt vohr‑duhn*
a trim	**bijknippen** *bie‑knih‑pehn*
Don't cut it too short.	**Niet te kort, alstublieft.**
	neet tuh kohrt ahls‑tew‑bleeft
Shorter here.	**Hier mag het korter.** *heer mahkh heht kohr‑tuhr*
I'd like…	**Ik wil graag…** *ihk vihl khraakh…*
an eyebrow/bikini wax	**een wenkbrauwwax/bikiniwax**
	uhn vehnk‑brow‑vahks/bee‑kee‑nee‑vahks
a facial	**een gezichtsbehandeling**
	uhn khuh‑zihkhts‑buh‑hahn‑duh‑lihng
a manicure/ pedicure	**een manicure/pedicure**
	uhn maa‑nee‑kewr/pay‑dee‑kewr
a (sports) massage	**een (sport)massage**
	uhn (spohrt)mah‑saa‑zhuh
Do you do…?	**Biedt u…?** *beet ew…*
acupuncture	**acupunctuur** *aa‑kew‑puhnk‑tewr*
aromatherapy	**aromatherapie** *aa‑roa‑maa‑tay‑raa‑pee*
oxygen treatment	**zuurstofbehandeling**
	zewr‑stohf‑buh‑hahn‑duh‑lihng
Is there a sauna?	**Is er een sauna?** *ihs ehr uhn sow‑naa*

Some luxury hotels in the Netherlands offer thalassotherapy, or sea water treatments, as well as other health and beauty treatments. A handful of day and destination spas are scattered through the country, for example near Rotterdam and Groningen.

Antiques

How old is this?	**Hoe oud is dit?**	*hoo owt ihs diht*
Will I have problems with customs?	**Krijg ik problemen met de douane?**	
	kriekh ihk proa·blay·muhn meht duh doo·vaa·nuh	
Do you have anything from the...period?	**Heeft u iets uit de ... periode?**	
	hayft ew eets awt duh ... pay·ree·yoa·deh	
Do I have to fill out any forms?	**Moet ik hier een formulier voor invullen?**	
	moot ihk heer uhn fohr·mew·leer foor ihn·fuh·lehn	
Is there a certificate of authenticity?	**Is er een certificaat van echtheid?**	
	ihs ehr uhn sehr·tee·fee·kaat fahn ehkht·hiet	
Can you ship/wrap it?	**Kunt u het verzenden/inpakken?**	
	kuhnt ew heht fehr·sehn·dehn/ihn·pah·kehn	

Clothing

I'd like...	**Ik wil graag...**	*ihk vihl khraakh...*
Can I try this on?	**Mag ik dit passen?**	*mahkh ihk diht pah·suhn*
It doesn't fit.	**Het past niet.**	*heht pahst neet*
It's too...	**Het is te...**	*heht ihs tuh...*
big	**groot**	*khroat*
small	**klein**	*klien*
short	**kort**	*kohrt*
long	**lang**	*lahng*
tight	**strak**	*strahk*
loose	**los**	*lohs*

| Do you have this in size…? | **Heeft u dit in maat…?** *hayft ew diht ihn maat…* |
| Do you have this in a bigger/smaller size? | **Heeft u dit in een grotere/kleinere maat?** *hayft ew diht ihn uhn khroa•tuh•ruh/ klie•nuh•ruh maat* |

For Numbers, see page 165.

YOU MAY HEAR…

Dat staat je goed. *daht staat yeh khoot*	That looks great on you.
Hoe zit het? *hoo ziht heht*	How does it fit?
Wij hebben het niet in uw maat. *wie heh•behn heht neet ihn ew maat*	We don't have your size.

YOU MAY SEE…

HERENKLEDING	men's clothing
DAMESKLEDING	women's clothing
KINDERKLEDING	children's clothing

Colors

I'd like something in...	**Ik wil graag iets...** *ihk vihl khraakh eets...*
beige	**in beige** *ihn beh•zhuh*
black	**zwarts** *zvahrts*
blue	**blauws** *blows*
brown	**bruins** *brawns*
green	**groens** *khroons*
gray	**grijs** *khries*
orange	**oranjes** *oa•rahn•yuhs*
pink	**in roze** *ihn roh•zuh*
purple	**paars** *paars*
red	**roods** *roats*
white	**wits** *vihts*
yellow	**geels** *khayls*

Clothes & Accessories

a backpack	**rugzak** *ruhkh•zahk*
a belt	**riem** *reem*
a bikini	**bikini** *bee•kee•nee*
a blouse	**bloes** *bloos*
a bra	**beha** *bay•haa*
a coat	**jas** *yahs*
a dress	**jurk** *yuhrk*
a hat	**hoed** *hoot*
a jacket	**jasje** *yahs•yuh*
jeans	**spijkerbroek** *spie•kuhr•brook*
pajamas	**pyjama** *pee•yaa•maa*
pants [trousers]	**lange broek** *lahng•uh brook*
pantyhose [tights]	**panty** *pehn•tee*
a purse [handbag]	**handtas** *hahn•tahs*

a raincoat	**regenjas** *ray·khuhn·yahs*
a scarf	**sjaal** *shaal*
a shirt	**overhemd?** *oa·fuhr·hehmt?*
shorts	**korte broek** *kohr·tuh brook*
a skirt	**rok** *rohk*
socks	**sokken** *soh·kuhn*
a suit	**pak** *pahk*
sunglasses	**zonnebril** *zoh·nuh·brihl*
a sweater	**trui** *traw*
a sweatshirt	**sweatshirt** *sweht·shuhrt*
swimming trunks	**zwembroek** *zwehm·brook*
a swimsuit	**zwempak** *zwehm·pahk*
a T-shirt	**T-shirt** *tee·shurt*
a tie	**stropdas** *strohp·dahs*
underwear	**slip** *m*/**onderbroek** *f slihp//ohn·duhr·brook*

Fabric

I'd like…	**Ik wil graag iets van…** *ihk vihl khraakh eets fahn…*
cotton	**katoen** *kaa·toon*
denim	**spijkerstof** *spie·kuhr·stohf*
lace	**kant** *kahnt*

leather	**leer** *layr*
linen	**linen** *lih·nuhn*
silk	**zijde** *zie·duh*
wool	**wol** *vohl*
Is it machine washable?	**Kan het in de machine worden gewassen?** *kahn heht ihn duh mah·shee·nuh vohr·duhn khuh·vahs·suhn*

Shoes

I'd like...	**Ik wil graag...** *ihk vihl khraakh...*
high-heels/flats	**hoge hakken/platte schoenen** *hoa·kheh hah·kehn/plah·teh skhoo·nehn*
boots	**laarzen** *laar·zuhn*
loafers	**moccasins** *moh·kah·sihns*
sandals	**sandalen** *sahn·daa·luhn*
shoes	**schoenen** *skhoo·nuhn*
slippers	**pantoffels** *pahn·toh·fuhls*
sneakers	**gymschoenen** *khihm·skhoo·nuhn*
In size...	**In maat...** *ihn maat...*

For Numbers, see page 165.

Sizes

small	**klein** *klien*
medium	**medium** *may·dee·yuhm*
large	**groot** *khroat*
extra large	**extra groot** *ehks·traa khroat*
petite	**tenger** *tehng·uhr*
plus size	**extra grote maat** *ehks·traa khroa·tuh maat*

Newsagent & Tobacconist

Do you sell English-language books/newspapers?	**Verkoopt u Engelstalige boeken/kranten?** *fuhr·koapt ew ehng·uhls·taa·lih·khuh boo·kuhn/krahn·tuhn*
I'd like...	**Ik wil graag...** *ihk vihl khraakh...*
candy [sweets]	**snoep** *snoop*
chewing gum	**wat kauwgom** *vaht kow·khohm*
a chocolate bar	**een chocoladereep** *ehn shoa·keh·laa·deh·rayp*
cigars	**wat sigaren** *vaht see·khaa·ruhn*
a pack/carton of cigarettes	**een pakje/slof sigaretten** *uhn pahk·yuh/slohf see·khaa·reh·tuhn*
a lighter	**een aansteker** *uhn aan·stay·kuhr*
a magazine	**een tijdschrift** *uhn tiet·skhrihft*
matches	**wat lucifers** *vaht lew·see·fehrs*
a newspaper	**een krant** *ehn krahnt*
a pen	**een pen** *ehn pehn*
a postcard	**een ansichtkaart** *ehn ahn·sihkht·kaart*
a road/town map of...	**een wegenkaart/stadsplattegrond van...** *uhn vay·khuhn·kaart/stahts·plah·tuh·khrohnt fahn...*
stamps	**wat postzegels** *vaht pohst·zay·khuhls*

Photography

I'm looking for... camera.	**Ik zoek...fototoestel.** *ihk zook...foa·toa·too·stehl*
an automatic	**een automatisch** *uhn oa·toa·maa·tees*
a digital	**een digital** *uhn dee·khee·taal*
a disposable	**een wegwerp** *uhn vehkh·wehrp*
I'd like...	**Ik wil graag...** *ihk vihl khraakh...*
a battery	**een batterij** *uhn bah·tuh·rie*
digital prints	**digitale afdrukken** *dee·khee·taa·luh ahf·druh·kuhn*
a memory card	**een geheugenkaart** *uhn khuh·hu·khuhn·kaart*
Can I print digital photos here?	**Kan ik hier digitale foto's afdrukken?** *kahn ihk heer dee·khee·taa·luh foa·toas ahf·druh·kuhn*

Souvenirs

decorative tiles	**siertegels** *seer·tay·khuhls*
(Gouda) candles	**(Goudse) kaarsen** *(khowt·suh) kaar·suhn*
cookies [biscuits]	**biscuits** *bihs·kvees*
bottle of wine	**fles wijn** *flehs vien*
box of chocolates	**doos bonbons** *doas bohn·bohns*
cheese	**kaas** *kaas*
chocolate	**chocolade** *shoa·koa·laa·duh*
clogs	**klompen** *klohm·puhn*
Delft blue pottery	**Delfts blauw** *dehlfts blow*
dolls in local costume	**poppen in klederdracht** *poh·puhn ihn klay·duhr·drahkht*
Dutch egg liqueur	**advocaat** *aht·foa·kaat*
Dutch gin	**jenever** *yuh·nay·fuhr*
key ring	**sleutelring** *slu·tuhl·rihng*

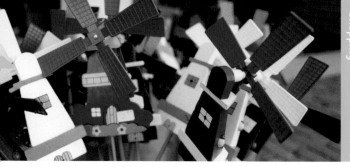

miniature windmill	**miniatuurmolen**
	mee•nee•yaa•tewr•moa•luhn
porcelain	**porselein** *pohr•suh•lien*
postcards	**ansichtkaarten** *ahn•sihkht•kaar•tuhn*
pottery	**aardewerk** *aar•duh•vehrk*
souvenir guide	**souvenirgids** *soo•fuh•neer•khihts*
Can I see this/that?	**Mag ik deze/die zien?**
	mahkh ihk day•zuh/dee zeen
It's the one in the window/display case.	**Het is die in de etalage/de vitrine.** *heht ihs dee ihn duh ay•taa•laa•zhuh/duh fee•tree•nuh*
I'd like…	**Ik wil graag…** *ihk vihl khraakh…*
a battery	**een batterij** *uhn bah•tuh•rie*
bracelet	**een armband** *uhn ahrm•bahnt*
a brooch	**een broche** *uhn broh•shuh*
earrings	**oorbellen** *oar•beh•luhn*
a necklace	**een halsketting** *uhn hahls•keh•tihng*
a ring	**een ring** *uhn rihng*
a watch	**een horloge** *uhn hohr•loa•zhuh*
I'd like…	**Ik wil graag iets…** *ihk vihl khraakh eets…*
copper	**van koper** *fahn koa•puhr*
crystal	**van kristal** *fahn krihs•tahl*

diamond	**van diamant**	*fahn dee·yaa·mahnt*
white/yellow gold	**van witgoud/geelgoud**	*fahn viht·khowt/ khayl·khowt*
pearls	**met parels**	*meht paa·ruhls*
pewter	**van tin**	*fahn tihn*
platinum	**van platina**	*fahn plaa·tee·naa*
sterling silver	**sterling zilver**	*stehr·lihng zihl·fuhr*
Is this real?	**Is dit echt?**	*ihs diht ehkht*
Can you engrave it?	**Kunt u het graveren?**	
	kuhnt ew heht khraa·fay·ruhn	

The Dutch are especially famous for their flowers and wooden clogs. Other original souvenirs include Delft blue (those not marked with a "D" are not genuine) and Makkum pottery, tiles, candles from Gouda, pewter and antiques (try around the Nieuwe Spiegelstraat in Amsterdam). Food items such as cheese (especially from Gouda or Edam), chocolate (Droste™) and cookies (Verkade™) are also popular. Souvenir shops tend to be expensive, but there are many specialty stores. Look for signs indicating tax-free shopping.

ESSENTIAL

When's the game?	**Wanneer is de wedstrijd?** *vah•nayr ihs duh veht•striet*	
Where's...?	**Waar is...?** *vaar ihs...*	
the beach	**het strand** *heht strahnt*	
the park	**het park** *heht pahrk*	
the pool	**het zwembad** *heht zvehm•baht*	
Is it safe to swim/ dive here?	**Is het veilig om hier te zwemmen/duiken?** *ihs heht fie•lihkh ohm heer tuh zveh•muhn/daw•kuhn*	
Can I rent [hire] golf clubs?	**Kan ik golfclubs huren?** *kahn ihk gohlf•kluhps hew•ruhn*	
What are the charges per hour?	**Hoeveel kost het per uur?** *hoo•fayl kohst heht pehr ewr*	
How far is it to...?	**Hoe ver is het naar...?** *hoo fehr ihs heht naar...*	
Can you show me on the map?	**Kunt u me dat op de kaart laten zien?** *kuhnt ew muh daht ohp duh kaart laa•tuhn zeen*	

Watching Sport

When's...?	**Wanneer is...?** *vah•nayr ihs...*
the basketball game	**de basketbalwedstrijd** *duh bahs•kuht•bahl•weht•striet*
the boxing match	**de bokswedstrijd** *duh bohks•weht•striet*
the cycling race	**de wielerwedstrijd** *duh vee•luhr•weht•striet*
the golf tournament	**het golftoernooi** *heht gohlf•toor•noay*

the soccer [football] game	**de voetbalwedstrijd** *duh foot·bahl·weht·striet*
the tennis match	**de tennismatch** *duh teh·nihs·mehtsh*
the volleyball game	**de volleybalwedstrijd** *duh voh·lee·bahl·weht·striet*
Which teams are playing?	**Welke teams spelen er?** *vehl·kuh teems spay·luhn ehr*
Where's…?	**Waar is…?** *vaar ihs…*
the horsetrack	**de paardenrenbaan** *duh paar·duhn·rehn·baan*
the racetrack	**het circuit** *heht suhr·kvee*
the stadium	**het stadion** *heht staa·dee·yohn*
Where can I place a bet?	**Waar kan ik gokken?** *waar kahn ihk khoh·kehn*

Cycling, both fietsen (leisure) and wielrennen (competitive), is very popular in the Netherlands. Other sports such as voetbal (soccer) and hockey (hockey) are also popular to watch and play. The Dutch are generally great fans of soccer and will wear the national color (orange) from head to toe while attending matches of the national soccer team.

Playing Sport

Where is/are…?	**Waar is/zijn…?** _vaar ihs/zien…_
the golf course	**de golfbaan** _duh gohlf·baan_
the gym	**de fitnessruimte** _duh fiht·nuhs·rawm·tuh_
the park	**het park** _heht pahrk_
the tennis courts	**de tennisbanen** _duh teh·nihs·baa·nuhn_
How much per…?	**Hoeveel kost het per…?** _hoo·fayl kohst heht pehr…_
day	**dag** _dahkh_
hour	**uur** _ewr_
game	**partij** _pahr·tie_
round	**ronde** _rohn·duh_
Can I rent [hire]…?	**Kan ik…huren?** _kahn ihk…hew·ruhn_
golf clubs	**golfclubs** _gohlf·kluhps_
equipment	**een uitrusting** _uhn awt·ruhs·tihng_
a racket	**een racket** _uhn rah·kuht_

At the Beach/Pool

Where's the beach/pool?	**Waar is het strand/zwembad?** _vaar ihs heht strahnt/zvehm·baht_
Is there…?	**Is er…?** _ihs ehr…_
a kiddie [paddling] pool	**een kinderzwembad** _uhn kihn·duhr·zvehm·baht_
an indoor/outdoor pool	**een binnenbad/buitenbad** _uhn bih·nuhn·baht/baw·tuhn·baht_
a lifeguard	**een badmeester** _uhn baht·mays·tuhr_
Is it safe…?	**Is het veilig…?** _ihs heht fie·lihkh…_
to swim	**om te zwemmen** _ohm tuh zveh·muhn_
to dive	**om te duiken** _ohm tuh daw·kuhn_
for children	**voor kinderen** _foar kihn·duh·ruhn_
I want to hire…	**Ik wil…huren.** _ihk vihl…hew·ruhn_
a deck chair	**een ligstoel** _uhn lihkh·stool_

diving equipment	**duikuitrusting** *dawk·awt·ruhs·tihng*
a jet-ski	**een jetski** *uhn dzheht·skee*
a motorboat	**een motorboot** *uhn moa·tohr·boat*
a rowboat	**een roeiboot** *uhn rooy·boat*
snorkeling equipment	**snorkeluitrusting** *snohr·kehl·awt·ruhs·tihng*
a surfboard	**een surfplank** *uhn suhrf·plangk*
a towel	**een handdoek** *uhn hahn·dook*
an umbrella	**een parasol** *uhn paa·raa·sohl*
water skis	**waterski's** *vaa·tuhr·skees*
a windsurfer	**een windsurfplank** *uhn vihnt·suhrf·plahnk*
For...hours.	**Voor...uur.** *foar...ewr*

For Traveling with Children, see page 143.

Zeilen (sailing) and other watersports are popular during the summer on Friese meren (the Frisian lakes) and in the more than 40 resorts along the coast. All different types of boats (including historic ships), canoes, windsurfers and water skis are available for rental. The Netherlands Board of Tourism publishes brochures with practical information and itineraries. Ask for information at the local tourist information office.

Winter Sports

A ticket for the skating rink, please.	**Een kaartje voor de ijsbaan, alstublieft.** *uhn kaart·yuh foar duh ies·baan ahls·tew·bleeft*
I want to rent [hire] ice skates.	**Ik wil schaatsen huren.** *ihk vihl skhaat·suhn hew·ruhn*
These are too big/small.	**Deze zijn te groot/klein.** *day·zuh zien tuh khroat/klien*
Can I take skating lessons?	**Kan ik schaatslessen nemen?** *ahn ihk skhaats·leh·suhn nay·muhn*
I'm a beginner.	**Ik ben beginner** *ihk behn beh·khih·nehr*
I'm experienced.	**Ik ben gevorderd** *ihk behn kheh·vohr·dehrt*

Out in the Country

I'd like a map of…	**Ik wil graag een kaart van…**
	ihk vihl khraakh uhn kaart fahn…
this region	**deze regio** *day·zuh ray·khee·oa*
the walking routes	**de wandelroutes** *duh vahn·duhl·roo·tuhs*
the bike routes	**de fietsroutes** *duh feets·roo·tuhs*
the trails	**de wandelpaden** *duh vahn·duhl·paa·duhn*
Is it easy/difficult?	**Is het makkelijk/moeilijk?**
	ihs heht mah·kuh·luhk/mooy·luhk
Is it far/steep?	**Is het ver/steil?** *ihs heht fehr/stiel*
How far is it to…?	**Hoe ver is het naar…?** *hoo fehr ihs heht naar…*
Can you show me	**Kunt u me dat op de kaart laten zien?**
on the map?	*kuhnt ew muh daht ohp duh kaart laa·tuhn zeen*
I'm lost.	**Ik ben verdwaald.** *ihk behn fuhr·dwaalt*
Where is…?	**Waar is…?** *vaar ihs…*
the bridge	**de brug** *duh bruhkh*
the cave	**de grot** *duh khroht*
the farm	**de boerderij** *duh boor·duh·rie*
the field	**het veld** *heht fehlt*
the forest	**het bos** *heht bohs*
the lake	**het meer** *heht mayr*
the nature preserve	**het natuurreservaat** *heht naa·tewr·ray·zuhr·faat*
the overlook	**het uitkijkpunt** *heht awt·kiek·puhnt*
the park	**het park** *heht pahrk*
the path	**het pad** *het paht*
the picnic area	**het picknickgebied** *heht pihk·nihk·khuh·beet*
the pond	**de vijver** *duh fie·fehr*
the river	**de rivier** *duh ree·feer*
the sea	**de zee** *duh zay*
the stream	**de beek** *duh bayk*

ESSENTIAL

What is there to do in the evenings?	**Wat is er 's avonds te doen?** *vaht ihs ehr saa•vohnts tuh doon*
Do you have a program of events?	**Heeft u een evenementenprogramma?** *hayft ew uhn ay•fuh•nuh•mehn•tuhn•proa•khrah•maa*
What's playing at the movies [cinema] tonight?	**Welke films draaien er vanavond?** *vehl•kuh fihlms draa•yuhn ehr fah•naa•fohnt*
Where's...?	**Waar is...?** *vaar ihs...*
the downtown area	**het stadscentrum** *heht staht•sehn•truhm*
the bar	**de bar** *duh bahr*
the dance club	**de discotheek** *duh dihs•koa•tayk*
Is there a cover charge?	**Moet ik entree betalen?** *moot ihk ahn•tray buh•taa•luhn*

The Netherlands has a strong tradition in the arts. There are hundreds of museums to be explored, many featuring work by famous Dutch artists such as Rembrandt, Van Gogh and Vermeer, to name a few. Price of admission varies, though some are free. Amsterdam is home to the national opera, ballet and theater companies, while The Hague and Rotterdam each have their own resident orchestras and dance companies. Cultural, musical and theater events are scheduled throughout the year; check with the tourist information office to see what's going on while you're in town.

Entertainment

Can you recommend...?	**Kunt u...aanbevelen?** *kuhnt ew...aan·buh·fay·luhn*
a concert	**een concert** *uhn kohn·sehrt*
a movie [film]	**een film** *uhn film*
an opera	**een opera** *uhn oa·puh·raa*
a play	**een toneelstuk** *uhn toa·nayl·stuhk*
When does it start/end?	**Wanneer begint/eindigt het?** *vah·nayr buh·khihnt/ien·dihkht heht*
What's the dress code?	**Zijn er kledingvoorschriften?** *zien ehr klay·dihng·foar·skhrihf·tuhn*
I really like...	**Ik hou erg van...** *ihk how ehrkh fahn...*
classical music	**klassieke muziek** *klah·see·kuh mew·zeek*
folk music	**volksmuziek** *fohlks·mew·zeek*
jazz	**jazz** *jehz*
pop music	**popmuziek** *pohp·mew·zeek*
rap	**rap** *rehp*

For Tickets, see page 19.

There are a number of festivals scheduled throughout the year in the Netherlands, some with moveable dates. The local tourist information office, hotels and guidebooks offer extensive information about local as well as national celebrations.

The biggest Dutch celebration every year across the country by far is **Koninginnedag** (Queen's Day). Celebrated on April 30th, when the weather in the Netherlands is mild, this giant open-air party features concerts and events, including the **vrijmarkt** (freemarket). **Koninginnedag** is the one day of the year when anyone is allowed to sell anything tax-free.

YOU MAY HEAR...

Zet uw mobiele telefoon uit.
zeht ew moa•bee•luh tay•luh•foan awt

Turn off your cell
[mobile] phones.

Nightlife

What is there to do in the evenings?	**Wat is er 's avonds te doen?** *vaht ihs ehr saa•vohnts tuh doon*
Can you recommend...?	**Kunt u...aanbevelen?** *kuhnt ew...aan•buh•fay•luhn*
a bar	**een bar** *uhn bahr*
a casino	**een casino** *uhn kaa•see•noa*
a club with Dutch music	**een club met Nederlandstalige muziek** *uhn klewp meht nay•dehr•lahnds•tah•lih•kheh mew•seek*
a dance club	**een discotheek** *uhn dihs•koa•tayk*
a gay club	**een homoclub** *uhn hoa•moa•club*
a jazz club	**een jazzclub** *uhn jehs•klewb*
a nightclub	**een nachtclub** *uhn nahkht•kluhp*
Is there live music?	**Is er livemuziek?** *ihs ehr laaif•mew•zeek*
How do I get there?	**Hoe kom ik er?** *hoo kohm ihk ehr*
Is there an admission charge?	**Moet ik entree betalen?** *moot ihk ahn•tray buh•taa•luhn*
Let's go dancing.	**Laten we gaan dansen.** *laa•tuhn vuh khaan dahn•suhn*
Is this area safe at night?	**Is dit gebied 's nachts veilig?** *ihs diht kheh•beet snahkhs fay•lihkh*

After dark, the Netherlands has a lot to offer depending on what you're in the mood for. In Amsterdam, the action is centered in three main areas. If you're looking for dance and night clubs, head to **Leidseplein**. For clubs, cabarets and strip shows, go to **Rembrandtplein**. The Red Light District is world-famous for offering a range of alternative activities.

For a low key evening, check out a 'brown' cafe (traditional Dutch bar), pub or bar. Amsterdam is home to about a thousand, so you can easily find one that fits your style.

Special Requirements

Business Travel

ESSENTIAL

I'm here on business.	**Ik ben hier voor zaken.**	*ihk behn heer foar zaa·kuhn*
Here's my business card.	**Hier is mijn visitekaartje.**	*heer ihs mien fee·<u>zee</u>·tuh·kaart·yuh*
Can I have your card?	**Mag ik uw visitekaartje?**	*mahkh ihk ew fee·zee·tuh·kaart·yuh*
I have a meeting with...	**Ik heb een afspraak met...**	*ihk hehp uhn ahf·spraak meht...*
Where's...?	**Waar is...?** *vaar ihs...*	
the business center	**het bedrijvencomplex heht** *buh·drie·fuhn·kohm·plehks*	
the convention hall	**het congresgebouw heht** *kohn·khrehs·khuh·bow*	
the meeting room	**de vergaderruimte** *duh fuhr·khaa·duhr·rawm·tuh*	

On Business

I'm here to attend...	**Ik ben hier voor...** *ihk behn heer foar...*	
a seminar	**een seminar** *uhn seh·mee·nahr*	
a conference	**een conferentie** *uhn kohn·fuh·rehnt·see*	
a meeting	**een vergadering** *uhn fuhr·khaa·duh·rihng*	
My name is...	**Mijn naam is...** *mien naam ihs...*	
May I introduce my colleague...?	**Mag ik mijn collega...voorstellen?** *mahkh ihk mien koh·lay·kha...foar·steh·luhn*	
I have a meeting/an appointment with...	**Ik heb een afspraak met...** *ihk hehp uhn ahf·spraak meht...*	
I'm sorry I'm late.	**Sorry dat ik te laat ben.** *soh·ree daht ihk tuh laat behn*	
I'd like an interpreter.	**Ik wil graag een tolk.** *ihk vihl khraag uhn tohlk*	
You can reach me at the...Hotel.	**U kunt me in hotel...bereiken.** *ew kuhnt muh ihn hoh·tehl...buh·rie·kuhn*	
I'm here until...	**Ik ben hier tot...** *ihk behn heer toht...*	

I need to...	**Ik wil...** *ihk vihl...*
make a call	**bellen** *beh·luhn*
make a photocopy	**iets kopiëren** *eets koa·pee·yay·ruhn*
send an e-mail	**een e-mail sturen** *uhn ee·mayl stew·ruhn*
send a fax	**een fax sturen** *uhn fahks stew·ruhn*
send a package (overnight)	**een pakketje (overnight) versturen** *uhn pah·keht·yuh (oa·fuhr·niet) fuhr·stew·ruhn*
It was a pleasure to meet you.	**Het was aangenaam om kennis met u te maken.** *heht wahs aan·khuh·naam ohm keh·nihs meht ew tuh maa·kuhn*

For Communications, see page 49.

The Dutch are hospitable people and pleasant to work with, but are also serious and direct in business dealings. Meetings tend to follow a strict agenda. Punctuality is taken seriously.

YOU MAY HEAR...

Heeft u een afspraak? *hayft ew uhn ahf·spraak* — Do you have an appointment?

Met wie? *meht vee* — With whom?

Hij *m*/**Zij** *f* **is in een vergadering.** *hie /zie ihs ihn uhn fuhr·khaa·duh·rihng* — He/She is in a meeting.

Een ogenblik, alstublieft. *uhn oa·khuhn·blihk ahls·tew·bleeft* — One moment, please.

Ga zitten. *khaa sih·tehn* — Have a seat.

Wilt u iets drinken? *wihlt ew eets drihn·kehn* — Would you like something to drink?

Bedankt voor uw komst. *buh·dangkt foar ew kohmst* — Thank you for coming.

Traveling with Children

ESSENTIAL

Is there a discount for children?	**Is er korting voor kinderen?** *ihs ehr kohr·tihng foar kihn·duh·ruhn*
Can you recommend a babysitter?	**Kunt u een oppas aanbevelen?** *kuhnt ew uhn ohp·pahs aan·buh·fay·luhn*
Can I have a highchair?	**Mogen we een kinderstoel?** *moa·khuhn vuh uhn kihn·duh·stool*
Where can I change the baby?	**Waar kan ik de baby verschonen?** *vaar kahn ihk duh bay·bee fuhr·skhoa·nuhn*

Out & About

Can you recommend something for the kids?	**Kunt u iets aanbevelen voor de kinderen?** *kuhnt ew eets aan·buh·fay·luhn foar duh kihn·duh·ruhn*
Where's...?	**Waar is...?** *vaar ihs...*
the amusement park	**het pretpark** *heht preht·pahrk*
Where's...?	**Waar is...?** *vaar ihs...*
the arcade	**de speelhal** *duh spayl·hahl*
the kiddie [paddling] pool	**het kinderzwembad** *heht kihn·duh·zvehm·baht*
the park	**het park** *heht pahrk*
the playground	**de speeltuin** *duh spayl·tawn*
the zoo	**de dierentuin** *duh dee·ruhn·tawn*
Are kids allowed?	**Zijn kinderen daar toegestaan?** *zien kihn·duh·ruhn daar too·khuh·staan*
Is it safe for kids?	**Is het veilig voor kinderen?** *ihs heht fie·lihkh foar kihn·duh·ruhn*

YOU MAY HEAR...

Wat schattig! *vaht skhah·tihkh* — How cute!

Hoe heet hij *m*/zij *f*? *hoo hayt hie/zie* — What's his/her name?

Hoe oud is hij *m* /zij *f*? *hoo owt ihs hie/zie* — How old is he/she?

Is it suitable for... year-olds?	**Is het geschikt voor kinderen van...jaar?** *ihs heht khuh·skhihkt foar kihn·duh·ruhn fahn...yaar*

For Numbers, see page 165.

Baby Essentials

Do you have...?	**Heeft u...?** *hayft ew...*
a baby bottle	**een babyfles** *uhn bay·bee·flehs*
baby wipes	**babydoekjes** *bay·bee·dook·yuhs*
a car seat	**een kinderzitje** *uhn kihn·duhr·ziht·yuh*
a children's menu/portion	**een kindermenu/kinderportie uhn** *kihn·duhr·muh·new/kihn·duhr·pohr·see*
a highchair	**een kinderstoel** *uhn kihn·duhr·stool*
a crib/cot	**een wieg/kinderbedje** *uhn veekh/kihn·duhr·beht·yuh*
diapers [nappies]	**luiers** *law·yuhrs*
formula	**flesvoeding** *flehs·foo·dihng*
a pacifier [dummy]	**een fopspeen uhn fohp·spayn**
a playpen	**een babybox** *uhn bay·bee·bohks*
a stroller [pushchair]	**een kinderwagen** *uhn kihn·duhr·vaa·khun*
Can I breastfeed the baby here?	**Mag ik mijn baby hier de borst geven?** *mahkh ihk mien bay·bee heer duh bohrst khay·fuhn*
Where can I change the baby?	**Waar kan ik de baby verschonen?** *vaar kahn ihk duh bay·bee fuhr·skhoa·nuhn*

For Dining with Children, see page 63.

Babysitting

Can you recommend a babysitter?	**Kunt u een oppas aanbevelen?** *kuhnt ew uhn ohp•pahs aan•buh•fay•luhn*
What's the charge?	**Hoeveel kost het?** *hoo•fayl kohst heht*
We'll be back by…	**We zijn om…uur terug.** *vuh zien ohm…ewr truhkh*
I can be reached at…	**U kunt me bij…bereiken.** *ew kuhnt muh bie…buh•rie•kuhn*

For Time, see page 166.

Health & Emergency

Can you recommend a pediatrician?	**Kunt u een kinderarts aanbevelen?** *kuhnt ew uhn kihn•duhr•ahrts aan•buh•fay•luhn*
My child is allergic to…	**Mijn kind is allergisch voor…** *mien kihnt ihs ah•lehr•khees foar…*
My child is missing.	**Ik ben mijn kind kwijt.** *ihk behn mien kihnt kviet*
Have you seen a boy/girl?	**Heeft u een jongen/meisje gezien?** *hayft ew uhn yohng•uhn/mies•yuh khuh•zeen*

For Meals & Cooking, see page 66.

For Health, see page 152.

For Police, see page 150.

Disabled Travelers

ESSENTIAL

Is there access for the disabled?	**Is het toegankelijk voor gehandicapten?** *is heht too·khahng·kuh·luhk foar khuh·hehn·dee·kehp·tuhn*
Is there a wheelchair ramp?	**Is er een rolstoeloprit?** *uhn rohl·stool·ohp·riht*
Is there a handicapped-[disabled-]accessible toilet?	**Is er een toilet dat toegankelijk is voor gehandicapten?** *uhn tvaa·leht daht too·khahng·kuh·luhk ihs foar khuh·hehn·dee·kehp·tuhn*
I need...	**Ik heb...nodig.** *ihk hehp...noa·dihkh*
assistance	**hulp** *huhlp*
an elevator [lift]	**een lift** *uhn lihft*
a ground-floor room	**een kamer op de begane grond** *uhn kaa·muhr ohp duh buh·khaa·nuh khrohnt*

Asking for Assistance

I'm disabled.	**Ik ben gehandicapt.** *ihk behn khuh·hehn·dee·kehpt*
I'm deaf.	**Ik ben doof.** *ihk behn doaf*
I'm visually/hearing impaired.	**Ik ben slechtziend/slechthorend.** *ihk behn slehkht·zeent/slehkht·hoa·ruhnt*
I'm unable to far/use the stairs.	**Ik kan niet ver lopen/de trap gebruiken.** *ihk kahn neet fehr loa·puhn/duh trahp khuh·braw·kuhn*
Please speak louder.	**Kunt u iets luider spreken, alstublieft?** *kuhnt ew eets law·dehr spray·kehn, ahls·tuh·bleeft*
Can I bring my wheelchair?	**Kan ik mijn rolstoel meenemen?** *kahn ihk mien rohl·stool may·nay·muhn*

Are guide dogs permitted?	**Zijn geleidehonden toegestaan?**
	zien khuh•lei•duh•hohn•duhn too•khuh•staan
Can you help me?	**Kunt u me helpen?** *kuhnt ew muh hehl•puhn*
Can you open/hold the door?	**Kunt u de deur openen/openhouden?**
	kuhnt ew duh dur oa•puh•nuhn/oa•puhn how•duhn

In An
Emergency

Emergencies

ESSENTIAL

Help!	**Help!** *hehlp*	
Go away!	**Ga weg!** *khaa vehkh*	
Stop thief!	**Houd de dief!** *howt duh deef*	
Get a doctor!	**Haal een dokter!** *haal uhn dohk•tuhr*	
Fire!	**Brand!** *brahnt*	
I'm lost.	**Ik ben verdwaald.** *ihk behn fuhr•dvaalt*	
Can you help me?	**Kunt u me helpen?** *kuhnt ew muh hehl•puhn*	

In an emergency, dial 112 for police, fire brigade or ambulance.

YOU MAY HEAR...

Vul dit formulier in. *fuhl diht fohr•muh•leer ihn* Fill out this form.

Mag ik uw legitimatiebewijs zien? Can I see your
mahkh ihk ew lay•khee•tee•maat•see zeen identification?

Wanneer/Waar is het gebeurd? When/Where did it
vah•nayr/vaar ihs heht khuh•burt happen?

Hoe ziet hij m/zij f eruit? What does he/
hoo zeet hie /zie ehr•awt she look like?

Police

ESSENTIAL

Call the police!	**Bel de politie!** *bel duh poa·leet·see*
Where's the police station?	**Waar is het politiebureau?** *vaar ihs heht poa·leet·see·bew·roa*
There's been an accident.	**Er heeft een ongeluk plaatsgevonden.** *ehr hayft uhn ohn·khuh·luhk plaats·khuh·fohn·duhn*
My child is missing.	**Ik ben mijn kind kwijt.** *ihk behn mien kihnt kviet*
I need...	**Ik wil...** *ihk vihl...*
an interpreter	**gebruikmaken van een tolk** *khuh·brawk maa·kuhn fahn uhn tohlk*
to contact my lawyer	**mijn advocaat spreken** *mien at·foa·kaat spray·kuhn*
to make a phone call	**iemand bellen** *ee·mahnt beh·luhn*
I'm innocent.	**Ik ben onschuldig.** *ihk behn ohn·skhuhl·dihkh*

Crime & Lost Property

I want to report...	**Ik wil...melden.** *ihk vihl... mehl·duhn*
a mugging	**een beroving** *uhn buh·roa·fihng*
a rape	**een verkrachting** *uhn fuhr·krahkh·tihng*
a theft	**een diefstal** *uhn deef·stahl*
I've been robbed/ mugged.	**Ik ben beroofd/overvallen.** *ihk behn buh·roaft/oa·fuhr·fah·luhn*
I've lost my...	**Ik heb mijn...verloren.** *ihk hehp mien...fuhr·loa·ruhn*

150

My…was/were stolen.	**Mijn…is/zijn gestolen.** *mien…ihs/zien khuh·stoa·luhn*
backpack	**rugzak** *ruhkh·zahk*
bicycle	**fiets** *feets*
camera	**fototoestel** *foa·toa·too·stehl*
car/hire car	**auto/huurauto** *ow·toa/hewr·ow·toa*
computer	**computer** *kohm·pyoo·tuhr*
credit card	**creditcard** *kreh·diht·kaart*
jewelry	**sieraden** *see·raa·duhn*
money	**geld** *khehlt*
purse [handbag]	**handtas** *hahn·tahs*
traveler's checks [cheques]	**reischeques** *ries·shehks*
wallet	**portemonnee** *pohr·tuh·moh·nay*

I need a police report. **Ik heb een politierapport nodig.**
ihk hehp uhn poa·lee·tsee·rah·pohrt noa·dihkh

Where is the British/ American/ Irish embassy? **Waar is de Britse/Amerikaanse/Ierse ambassade?**
waar ihs duh briht·se/aa·meh·ree·kaan·seh/eer·seh ahm·bah·saa·duh

Health

ESSENTIAL

I'm sick [ill].	**Ik ben ziek.** *ihk behn zeek*
I need an English-speaking doctor.	**Ik zoek een dokter die Engels spreekt.** *ihk zook uhn dohk•tuhr dee ehng•uhls spraykt*
It hurts here.	**Het doet hier pijn.** *heht doot heer pien*
I have a stomachache.	**Ik heb maagpijn.** *ihk hehp maakh•pien*

Finding a Doctor

Can you recommend a doctor/dentist?	**Kunt u een dokter/tandarts aanbevelen?** *kuhnt ew uhn dohk•tuhr/tahnt•ahrts aan•buh•fay•luhn*
Can the doctor come to see me here?	**Kan de dokter naar mij toekomen?** *kahn duh dohk•tuhr naar mie too•koa•muhn*
I need an English-speaking doctor.	**Ik heb een Engelsprekende dokter nodig.** *ihk hehp uhn ehng•ehls•spray•kehn•duh dohk•tehr noa•dihhk*
What are the office hours?	**Wat zijn de openingstijden?** *vaht zien duh oa•puh•nihngs•tie•duhn*
Can I make an appointment for today/tomorrow ?	**Kan ik een afspraak maken voor vandaag/morgen?** *kahn ihk uhn ahf•spraak maa•kuhn foar fahn•daakh/mohr•khuhn*
I'd like an appointment for as soon as possible.	**Ik wil zo snel mogelijk een afspraak maken.** *ihk wihl soa snehl moa•kheh•lehk uhn ahf•spraak maa•ken*
It's urgent.	**Het is dringend.** *heht ihs drihng•uhnt*

Symptoms

I'm...	**Ik...** *ihk...*
bleeding	**bloed** *bloot*
constipated	**heb last van constipatie**
	hehp lahst fahn kohn·stee·paat·see
dizzy	**ben duizelig** *behn daw·zuh·luhkh*
nauseous	**ben misselijk** *behn mih·suh·luhk*
vomiting	**moet overgeven** *moot oa·fuhr·khay·fuhn*
It hurts here.	**Het doet hier pijn.** *heht doot heer pien*
I have...	**Ik heb...** *ihk hehp...*
an allergic reaction	**een allergische reactie uhn**
	ah·lehr·khee·suh ray·ahk·see
chest pain	**pijn op mijn borst** *pien ohp mien bohrst*
cramps	**kramp** *krahmp*
diarrhea	**diarree** *dee·yaa·ray*
an earache	**oorpijn** *oar·pien*
a fever	**koorts** *koarts*
pain	**pijn** *pien*
a rash	**huiduitslag** *hawt·awt·slahkh*
a sore throat	**keelpijn** *kayl·pien*
a sprain	**iets verstuikt** *eets fuhr·stawkt*

a stomachache	**maagpijn** *maakh•pien*
I have some swelling.	**Het is opgezet.** *heht ihs ohp•khuh•zeht*
I've been sick [ill] for...days.	**Ik ben al...dagen ziek.** *ihk behn ahl...daa•khuhn zeek*

For Numbers, see page 165.

Conditions

I'm anemic.	**Ik heb bloedarmoede.** *ihk hehp bloot•ahr•moo•duh*
I'm diabetic.	**Ik ben suikerpatiënt.** *ihk behn saw•kuhr•paa•shehnt*
I'm epileptic.	**Ik heb epilepsie.** *ihk hehp ay•pee•lehp•see*
I have asthma.	**Ik heb astma.** *ihk hehp ahs•maa*
I'm allergic to antibiotics/penicillin.	**Ik ben allergisch voor antibiotica/penicilline.** *ihk behn ah•lehr•khees foar ahn•tee•bee•oa•tee•kaa/pay•nee•see•lee•nuh*
I have...	**Ik heb...** *ihk hehp...*
arthritis	**artritis** *ahrt•ree•tihs*
high/low blood pressure	**hoge/lage bloeddruk** *hoa•khuh/laa•khuh bloot•druhk*
a heart condition	**een hartkwaal** *uhn hahrt•kvaal*
I'm on...	**Ik neem...** *ihk naym...*

YOU MAY HEAR...

Wat is er mis? *vaht ihs ehr mihs* — What's wrong?

Waar doet het pijn? *vaar doot heht pien* — Where does it hurt?

Doet het hier pijn? *doot huht heer payn* — Does it hurt here?

Neemt u andere medicijnen? *naymt ew ahn·duh·ruh may·dee·sie·nuhn* — Are you taking any other medication?

Bent u ergens allergisch voor? *behnt ew ehr·khuhns ah·lehr·khees foar* — Are you allergic to anything?

Kunt u uw mond openen? *kuhnt ew ewv mohnt oa·puh·nuhn* — Open your mouth.

Even diep ademhalen. *ay·fuhn deep aa·duhm·haa·luhn* — Breathe deeply.

Hoesten, alstublieft. *hoos·tehn, ahls·tuh·bleeft* — Cough, please.

Ga naar het ziekenhuis. *khaa naar huht see·kehn·haws* — Go to the hospital.

Treatment

Do I need a prescription/medicine? **Heb ik een recept/medicijn nodig?** *hehp ihk uhn reh·sehpt/may·dee·sien noa·dihkh*

Can you prescribe a generic drug [unbranded medication]? **Kunt u een standaard medicijn voorschrijven** *kuhnt ew uhn stahn·daart may·dee·sien foar·skhrie·fehn*

Where can I get it? **Waar kan ik dit krijgen?** *waar kahn ihk diht krie·khehn*

For What to Take, see page 159.

Hospital

Can you notify my family?	**Kunt u mijn familie op de hoogte brengen?** *kuhnt ew mien faa•mee•lee ohp duh hoakh•tuh brehng•uhn*
I'm in pain.	**Ik heb pijn.** *ik hehp pien*
I need a doctor/nurse.	**Ik heb een dokter/verpleegster nodig.** *ihk hehp uhn dohk•tuhr/fuhr•playkh•stuhr noa•dihkh*
When are visiting hours?	**Wanneer is het bezoekuur?** *vah•nayr ihs heht buh•zook•ewr*
I'm visiting...	**Ik kom op bezoek bij...** *ihk kohm ohp buh•zook bie...*

Dentist

I've broken a tooth/ lost a filling.	**Ik heb een tand gebroken/ben een vulling verloren.** *ihk hehp uhn tahnt khuh•broa•kuhn/behn uhn fuh•lihng fuhr•loa•ruhn*
I have toothache.	**Ik heb kiespijn.** *ihk hehp kees•pien*
Can you fix this denture?	**Kunt u dit kunstgebit repareren?** *kuhnt ew diht kuhnst•khuh•biht ray•paa•ray•ruhn*

Gynecologist

I have menstrual cramps/a vaginal infection.	**Ik heb menstruatiepijn/een vaginale infectie.** *ihk hehp mehn•strew•aat•see•pien/uhn faa•khih•naa•luh ihn•fehk•see*
I missed my period.	**Ik ben niet ongesteld geworden.** *ihk behn neet ohn•khuh•stehlt khuh•vohr•duhn*
I'm on the Pill.	**Ik ben aan de pil.** *ihk behn aan duh pihl*
I'm (not) pregnant.	**Ik ben (niet) zwanger.** *ihk behn (neet) zvahng•uhr*
I'm (...months) pregnant.	**Ik ben (...maanden) zwanger.** *ihk behn (...maandehn) swahng•ehr*

| I haven't had my period for...months. | **Ik ben al...maanden niet ongesteld geweest.** *ihk behn ahl...maan•duhn neet ohn•khuh•stehlt khuh•vayst* |

For Numbers, see page 165.

Optician

I've lost...	**Ik heb...verloren.** *ihk hehp...fuhr•loa•ruhn*
a contact lens	**een van mijn contactlenzen** *ayn fahn mien kohn•tahkt•lehn•zuhn*
my glasses	**mijn bril** *mien brihl*
a lens	**een lens** *uhn lehns*

Payment & Insurance

How much?	**Hoeveel kost het?** *hoo•fayl kohst heht*
Can I pay by credit card?	**Kan ik met een creditcard betalen?** *kahn ihk meht uhn khreh•diht•kaart buh•taa•luhn*
I have insurance.	**Ik ben verzekerd.** *ihk behn fuhr•zay•kuhrt*
Can I have a receipt for my insurance?	**Mag ik een kwitantie hebben voor mijn verzekering?** *mahkh ihk uhn kvee•tahnt•see heh•buhn foar mien fuhr•zay•kuh•rihng*

Pharmacy

ESSENTIAL

Where's the nearest pharmacy [chemist]?	**Waar is de dichtstbijzijnde apotheek?** *vaar ihs duh dihkhtst•bie•zien•duh ah•poa•tayk*
What time does the pharmacy [chemist] open/close?	**Hoe laat gaat de apotheek open/dicht?** *hoo laat khaat duh ah•poa•tayk oa•puhn/dihkht*
What would you recommend for…?	**Wat zou u aanbevelen voor…?** *vaht zow ew aan•buh•fay•luhn foar…*
How much should I take?	**Hoeveel moet ik er innemen?** *hoo•fayl moot ihk ehr ihn•nay•muhn*
Can you fill [make up] this prescription for me?	**Kunt u dit recept voor me klaarmaken?** *kuhnt ew diht ruh•sehpt foar muh klaar•maa•kuhn*
I'm allergic to…	**Ik ben allergisch voor…** *ihk behn ah•lehr•khees foar…*

The **apotheek** (pharmacy) fills medical prescriptions and the **drogisterij** (drug store) sells non-prescription items, toiletries and cosmetics. Regular opening hours are Monday to Friday from 8:00 or 9:00 a.m. until 6:00 p.m. On nights and weekends, pharmacies open on a rotating schedule: if the one you are outside is closed, check the sign in the window to find the closest pharmacy that is open.

What to Take

How much should I take?	**Hoeveel moet ik er innemen?** *hoo•fayl moot ihk ehr ihn•nay•muhn*
How often?	**Hoe vaak per dag?** *hoo•faak pehr dahk*
Is it suitable for children?	**Is het geschikt voor kinderen?** *ihs heht khuh•skhihkt foar kihn•duh•ruhn*
I'm taking...	**Ik neem...** *ihk naym...*
Are there side effects?	**Zijn er bijwerkingen?** *zien ehr bie•vehr•kihng•uhn*
I'd like some medicine for...	**Ik wil graag medicijnen tegen...** *ihk vihl khraakh may•dee•sie•nuhn tay•khuhn...*
a cold	**verkoudheid** *fuhr•kowt•hiet*
a cough	**hoesten** *hoos•tuhn*
diarrhea	**diarree** *dee•ah•ray*
a headache	**hoofdpijn** *hoaft•payn*
insect bites	**insectensteek** *ihn•sehk•tehn•stayk*
motion sickness	**reisziekte** *ries•zeek•tuh*
a sore throat	**keelpijn** *kayl•pien*
sunburn	**zonnebrand** *zoh•nuh•branht*
a toothache	**kiespijn** *kees•payn*
an upset stomach	**maagpijn** *maakh•pien*

YOU MAY SEE...

EEN/DRIE KEER PER DAG	once/three times a day
TABLETTEN	tablets
DRUPPEL	drop
VOOR/NA/BIJ MAALTIJDEN	before/after/with meals
OP EEN LEGE MAAG	on an empty stomach
IN EEN KEER DOORSLIKKEN	swallow whole
NIET INNEMEN	do not ingest

Basic Supplies

I'd like...	**Ik wil graag...** *ihk vihl khraakh...*
acetaminophen [paracetamol]	**paracetamol** *paa·raa·say·taa·mohl*
antiseptic cream	**antiseptische crème** *ahn·tee·sehp·tee·suh kreh·muh*
I'd like...	**Ik wil graag...** *ihk vihl khraakh...*
aspirin	**aspirine** *ahs·pee·ree·nuh*
bandages [plasters]	**pleisters** *plies·tuhrs*
a comb	**een kam** *uhn kahm*
condoms	**condooms** *kohn·doams*
contact lens solution	**contactlensvloeistof** *kohn·tahkt·lehns·flooy·stohf*
deodorant	**deodorant** *day·oa·doa·rahnt*
a hairbrush	**een haarborstel** *uhn haar·bohr·stehl*
hair spray	**haarspray** *haar·spray*
ibuprofen	**ibuprofen** *ee·bew·proa·fehn*
insect repellent	**insektenspray** *ihn·sehk·tuhn·spray*

lotion	**lotion** *lotion*	
a nail file	**een nagelvijl** *uhn naa·khuhl·fiel*	
(disposable)		
razors	**wegwerpscheermesjes** *vehkh·vehrp·skhayr·mehs·yuhs*	
razor blades	**scheermesjes** *skhayr·mehs·yuhs*	
sanitary napkins	**maandverband**	
[pads]	*maant·fuhr·bahnt*	
shampoo/	**shampoo/conditioner**	
conditioner	*shahm·poa/kohn·dih·shuh·nuhr*	
soap	**zeep** *zayp*	
sunscreen	**zonnebrandcrème** *zoh·nuh·brahnt·kreh·muh*	
tampons	**tampons** *tahm·pohns*	
tissues	**tissues** *tih·shoos*	
toilet paper	**toiletpapier** *tvaa·leht·paa·peer*	
a toothbrush	**een tandenborstel** *uhn tahn·duhn·bohr·stuhl*	
toothpaste	**tandpasta** *tahnt·pahs·taa*	

For Baby Essentials, see page 144.

The Basics

Grammar

Regular Verbs

All regular Dutch verbs follow the same conjugation pattern in the present tense: add -t to the verb root in the second and third person singular (unless the verb ends in t), and add **-en** to the verb root in all plural forms. The past tense of regular verbs is formed by adding **-te(n)** or **-de(n)** to the root. The future tense consists of the auxiliary verb **zullen** (will) + infinitive. Below are the present, past and future forms of the regular verb **werken** (to work).

WERKEN (to work)		Present	Past	Future
I	ik	werkt	werkte	zal werken
you (sing., for./inf.)	u/jij	werkt	werkte	zal werken
he/she	hij/zij	werkt	werkte	zal werken
we	wij	werken	werkten	zullen werken
you (pl.)	jullie	werken	werkten	zullen werken
they	zij	werken	werkten	zullen werken

for. = formal inf. = informal pl. = plural sing. = singular

Irregular Verbs

There are numerous irregular verbs in Dutch. These must be memorized. Below are the present tense conjugations for the frequently used verbs **hebben** (to have) and **zijn** (to be).

		HEBBEN (to have)	ZIJN (to be)
I	ik	heb	ben
you (sing., for./inf.)	u/jij	heeft/hebt	bent

		HEBBEN (to have)	ZIJN (to be)
he/she	hij/zij	heeft	is
we	wij	hebben	zijn
you (pl.)	jullie	hebben	zijn
they	zij	hebben	zijn

Nouns & Articles

Nouns are either masculine m, feminine f, or neuter. Masculine and feminine nouns take the definite article **de**, neuter nouns take h**et**. All nouns take the indefinite article **een** (a/an).

The plural is generally formed by adding **en**; most nouns ending with **je**, **el**, **em**, **en** and **aar** take **s**. For a few nouns, the plural is formed by adding **'s**:

de deur (the door), **de deuren** (the doors)

het huis (the house), de huizen (the houses)

het café (the cafe), **de cafés** (the cafes)

de bikini (the bikini), **de bikini's** (the bikini's)

Word Order

Word order in Dutch is generally as in English, i.e. subject-verb-object.

De man zoekt de fiets. The man searches for the bike.

Questions can be formed in Dutch:

1. by inverting the subject and verb:

Kunt u me helpen? Can you help me?

2. by using a question word + the inverted order:

Waar ben je? Where are you?

Negation

To negate a statement, place **niet** (not) after the verb, or after the object.

Ik rook niet. I don't smoke.

Ik heb de kaartjes niet. I don't have the tickets.

For nouns, the negation is made by adding **geen.**

Ik heb geen sigaretten. I have no cigarettes.

Imperatives

In Dutch, the imperative is derived from the second person plural or singular (you) form in the present tense. When using the imperative with we, add **laten** (let) + the infinitive, as in English.

you (inf.)	**Ga! (Go!)**
you (pl., inf.)	**Ga! (Go!)**
you (for.)	**Gaat! (Go!)**
we	**Laten we gaan! (Let's go!)**

Comparatives & Superlatives

In Dutch the comparative of an adjective is usually formed by adding **-er** to the end of the adjective. Examples:

klein **(small)**   kleiner **(smaller)**

The superlative of an adjective is usually formed by adding **-st** to the end of the adjective. **Examples:**

klein (small)   **kleinst** (smallest)

Adjectives

Adjectives usually end with an **e** (with the exception of a singular neuter noun), for example:

de kleine jongen (the small boy)

However, **e** is not added when the adjective follows the noun, or when the noun is preceded by **elk/ieder** (each), **veel** (much), **zulk** (such) and **geen** (no). **Examples:**

de jongen is klein (the boy is small)

geen warm water (no warm water)

Adverbs & Adverbial Expressions

In Dutch, adverbs are usually identical to the adjectives but, unlike adjectives, their endings don't change. **Examples:**

Adjective: **het lekkere eten** the good food

Adverb: **het eten is lekker** the food is good

Numbers

ESSENTIAL

0	**nul**	*nuhl*
1	**één**	*ayn*
2	**twee**	*tvay*
3	**drie**	*dree*
4	**vier**	*feer*
5	**vijf**	*fief*
6	**zes**	*zehs*
7	**zeven**	*zay·fuhn*
8	**acht**	*ahkht*
9	**negen**	*nay·khuhn*
10	**tien**	*teen*
11	**elf**	*ehlf*
12	**twaalf**	*tvaalf*
13	**dertien**	*dehr·teen*
14	**veertien**	*fayr·teen*
15	**vijftien**	*fief·teen*
16	**zestien**	*zehs·teen*
17	**zeventien**	*zay·fuhn·teen*
18	**achttien**	*ahkh·teen*
19	**negentien**	*nay·khuhn·teen*
20	**twintig**	*tvihn·tuhkh*
21	**eenentwintig**	*ayn·uhn·tvihn·tuhkh*
22	**tweeëntwintig**	*tvay·uhn·tvihn·tuhkh*
30	**dertig**	*dehr·tihkh*
31	**eenendertig**	*ayn·uhn·dehr·tihkh*
40	**veertig**	*fayr·tihkh*
50	**vijftig**	*fief·tihkh*

60	**zestig** *zehs·tihkh*
70	**zeventig** *zay·fuhn·tihkh*
80	**tachtig** *tahkh·tikh*
90	**negentig** *nay·khuhn·tihkh*
100	**honderd** *hohn·duhrt*
101	**honderdéén** *hohn·duhrt·ayn*
200	**tweehonderd** *tvay·hohn·duhrt*
500	**vijfhonderd** *fief·hohn·duhrt*
1,000	**duizend** *daw·zuhnt*
10,000	**tienduizend** *teen·daw·zuhnt*
1,000,000	**één miljoen** *uhn mihl·yoon*

Ordinal Numbers

first	**eerste** *ayr·stuh*
second	**tweede** *tvay·duh*
third	**derde** *dehr·duh*
fourth	**vierde** *feer·duh*
fifth	**vijfde** *fief·duh*
once	**één keer** *ayn kayr*
twice	**twee keer** *tvay kayr*
three times	**drie keer** *dree kayr*

Time

ESSENTIAL

What time is it?	**Hoe laat is het?** *hoo laat ihs heht*
It's noon [midday].	**Het is twaalf uur 's middags.**
	heht ihs tvaalf ewr smih·dahkhs
At midnight.	**Om middernacht.** *ohm mih·duhr·nahkht*

From nine o'clock to 5 o'clock.	**Van negen tot vijf.** *fahn nay•khuhn toht fief*	
Twenty after [past] four.	**Tien voor half vijf.** *teen foar hahlf fief*	
A quarter to nine.	**Kwart voor negen.** *kvahrt foar nay•khuhn*	
5:30 a.m./p.m.	**Half zes 's morgens/Half zes 's avonds.** *hahlf zehs smohr•khuhns/hahlf zehs saa•fohnts*	

Days

ESSENTIAL

Monday	**maandag** <u>maan</u>•dahkh
Tuesday	**dinsdag** <u>dihns</u>•dahkh
Wednesday	**woensdag** <u>voons</u>•dahkh
Thursday	**donderdag** <u>dohn</u>•duhr•dahkh
Friday	**vrijdag** <u>frie</u>•dahkh
Saturday	**zaterdag** <u>zaa</u>•tuhr•dahkh
Sunday	**zondag** <u>zohn</u>•dahkh

Dates

yesterday	**gisteren** <u>khihs</u>•tuh•ruhn
today	**vandaag** fahn•<u>daakh</u>
tomorrow	**morgen** <u>mohr</u>•khuhn
day	**dag** dahkh
week	**week** vayk
month	**maand** maant
year	**jaar** yaar

Months

January	**januari** _yah_•new•aa•ree
February	**februari** _fay_•brew•aa•ree
March	**maart** maart
April	**april** ah•_prihl_
May	**mei** mie
June	**juni** _yew_•nee
July	**juli** yew•lee
August	**augustus** ow•_khuhs_•tuhs
September	**september** sehp•_tehm_•buhr
October	**oktober** ohk•_toa_•buhr
November	**november** noa•_fehm_•buhr
December	**december** day•_sehm_•buhr

Seasons

spring	**de lente** duh _lehn_•tuh
summer	**de zomer** duh _zoa_•muhr
fall [autumn]	**de herfst** duh hehrfst
winter	**de winter** duh _vihn_•tuhr

Holidays

January 1	**Nieuwjaarsdag** New Year's Day
April 30	**Koninginnedag** Queen Mother's Birthday
May 4	**Dodenherdenking** Remembrance Day, World War II
May 5	**Bevrijdingsdag** Liberation Day
December 25	**Eerste kerstdag** Christmas Day
December 26	**Tweede kerstdag** Boxing Day

Moveable Dates

Good Friday	**Goede Vrijdag**
Easter	**Pasen**
Ascension	**Hemelvaartsdag**
Pentecost	**Pinksteren**

Conversion Tables

When you know	Multiply by	To find
ounces	*28.3*	grams
pounds	*0.45*	kilograms
inches	*2.54*	centimeters
feet	*0.3*	meters
miles	*1.61*	kilometers
square inches	*6.45*	sq. centimeters
square feet	*0.09*	sq. meters
square miles	*2.59*	sq. kilometers
pints (U.S./Brit)	*0.47/0.56*	liters
gallons (U.S./Brit)	*3.8/4.5*	liters
Fahrenheit	*5/9, after −32*	Centigrade
Centigrade	*9/5, then +32*	Fahrenheit

Kilometers to Miles Conversions

1 km – 0.62 mi	**20 km** – 12.4 mi
5 km – 3.10 mi	**50 km** – 31.0 mi
10 km – 6.20 mi	**100 km** – 61.0 mi

Measurement

1 gram	**gram** *khrahm*	= 0.035 oz.
1 kilogram (kg)	**kilogram** *kee•loa•<u>khrahm</u>*	= 2.2 lb
1 liter (l)	**liter** <u>*lee*</u>*•tuhr*	= 1.06 U.S/0.88 Brit. quarts
1 centimeter (cm)	**centimeter** *sehn•tee• may•tuhr*	= 0.4 inch
1 meter (m)	**meter** <u>*may*</u>*•tuhr*	= 3.28 ft.
1 kilometer (km)	**kilometer** *kee•<u>loa</u>•may•tuhr*	= 0.62 mile

Temperature

-40° C	–	-40° F
-30° C	–	-22° F
-20° C	–	-4° F
-10° C	–	14° F
-5° C	–	23° F
-1° C	–	30° F
0° C	–	32° F
5° C	–	41° F
10° C	–	50° F
15° C	–	59° F
20° C	–	68° F
25° C	–	77° F
30° C	–	86° F
35° C	–	95° F

Oven Temperature

100° C – 212° F	**177° C** – 350° F
121° C – 250° F	**204° C** – 400° F
149° C – 300° F	**260° C** – 500° F

Dictionary

A

about (approximately) ongeveer;
  (regarding) over
above boven
abroad in het buitenland
accept accepteren
access toegang
accident ongeluk
accidentally per ongeluk
accommodations logies
accompany meegaan
acetaminophen paracetamol
acne acne
across naar de overkant
acupuncture acupunctuur
adapter adapter
additional extra
address adres
adjoining aangrenzend
admission charge toegangsprijs
adult volwassene
after na
afternoon middag
aftershave aftershave
agree akkoord gaan
air lucht
air conditioning airco
air mattress luchtbed
air pump luchtpomp
airmail luchtpost
airport vliegveld
airsickness luchtziekte
aisle gangpad
alarm clock wekker
all alle

allergic allergisch
allergy allergie
alley steegje
all-night pharmacy nachtapotheek
allow toestaan
allowance (quantity) toegestane
  hoeveelheid; **(permit)** vergunning
almost bijna
alone alleen
already al
also ook
alter vermaken
alternate adj alternatief
aluminum foil aluminiumfolie
always altijd
amazing verbazingwekkend
ambassador ambassadeur
ambulance ambulance
American n Amerikaan;
  adj Amerikaans
amount (money) bedrag;
  (quantity) hoeveelheid
amusement park pretpark
anesthetic verdovingsmiddel
and en
anemia bloedarmoede
animal dier
another een ander
antacid antacidum
antibiotics antibiotica
antifreeze antivries
antique antiek
antiseptic adj antiseptisch
any wat
anyone iemand

---

adj adjective	**BE** British English	**prep** preposition
adv adverb	**n** noun	**v** verb

anything iets
apartment appartement
apologize zich verontschuldigen
appendix blindedarm
appetite eetlust
appointment afspraak
approve goedkeuren
approximately ongeveer
arcade speelhal
area code netnummer
arm arm
aromatherapy aromatherapie
around rond
arrivals (airport) aankomst
arrive arriveren
art gallery kunstgalerie
arthritis artritis
ashtray asbak
ask vragen
aspirin aspirine
assistance hulp
asthma astma
at (time) om; **(place)** op
ATM geldautomaat
attack aanval
attractive aantrekkelijk
audio guide audiogids
aunt tante
Australia Australië
authentic authentiek
authenticity echtheid
automatic (car) automaat
available (seat) vrij;
  (general) beschikbaar
away *adv* weg
awful afschuwelijk

B
baby baby
baby bottle zuigfles

baby food babyvoeding
baby wipes babydoekjes
babysitter oppas
back (body part) rug;
(not front) achterkant
backache rugpijn
backpack rugzak
bad slecht
bag tas
baggage [BE] bagage
baggage claim bagageafhaalruimte
bake bakken
bakery bakker
balcony balkon
ball bal
ballet ballet
band band
bandage (small) pleister;
  (large) verband
bank bank
bank charges bankkosten
bar bar
barber herenkapper
bargain koopje
barrier barrière
baseball honkbal
basement kelder
basket mand
basketball basketbal
bath bad
bathroom (bath/shower)
badkamer; **(restroom)** toilet
battery (general) batterij; **(car)** accu
battlesite slagveld
be zijn
beach strand
beautiful mooi
because omdat
become worden

bed bed
bed and breakfast logies en ontbijt
bedding beddengoed
bedroom slaapkamer
before voor
begin beginnen
beginner beginner
behind achter
Belgium België
belong toebehoren
belt riem
bet wedden
between tussen
beware oppassen
bib slabbetje
bicycle fiets
big groot
bike path fietspad
bikini bikini
bill *n* rekening
binoculars verrekijker
bird vogel
birthday verjaardag
bite (general) beet; **(insect)** beet;
  v bijten
bitter bitter
bizarre bizar
bladder blaas
blanket deken
bleach bleekmiddel
bleed bloeden
blister blaar
blocked (drain) verstopt;
  (road) versperd
blood bloed
blood group bloedgroep
blood pressure bloeddruk
blouse bloes
blow dry föhnen

blue blauw
board *v* boarden
boarding card instapkaart
boat trip boottocht
bone bot
book boek
bookstore boekwinkel
boots laarzen
boring saai
born geboren
borrow lenen
botanical garden botanische tuin
bother *v* lastigvallen
bottle fles
bottle opener flesopener
boulevard boulevard
bowel darm
bowl kom
box doos
boxing boksen
boy jongen
boyfriend vriend
bra beha
bracelet armband
brake rem
break *v* breken
break down (car) pech hebben;
  (appliance) defect raken
breakfast ontbijt
breast borst
breastfeed borst geven
breathe ademhalen
bridge brug
bring brengen
British *n* Britten; *adj* Brits
brochure brochure
broken (body part or thing)
  gebroken; **(thing)** kapot
bronchitis bronchitis

brooch broche
broom bezem
bruise blauwe plek
bucket emmer
bug insect
building gebouw
build *v* bouwen
bulletin board mededelingenbord
burn brandwond
bus bus
bus lane busbaan
bus route busroute
bus shelter bushokje
bus station busstation
bus stop bushalte
bus ticket strippenkaart
business zaken
business card visitekaartje
business center bedrijvencomplex
business class businessclass
business district zakendistrict
busy druk
but maar
butane gas butagas
butcher slager
button knoop
buy kopen
by (near) bij; **(time)** niet later dan
bye (also used at arrival) dag;
  (only at departure) tot ziens

C

cabin hut
cafe café
calendar kalender
call *n* gesprek; **(phone)** *v* bellen;
  (name) *v* heten
calorie calorie
camera fototoestel
camp *v* kamperen

campsite camping
can (may) mogen;
(be able) kunnen
can opener blikopener
Canada Canada
canal (general) kanaal;
(in city) gracht
cancel annuleren
cancer kanker
candle kaars
canoeing kanovaren
cap (hat) pet; **(dental)** kroon
capsule (medication) capsule
car (vehicle) auto;
(train compartment) wagon
car deck (ferry) autodek
car hire [BE] autoverhuurbedrijf
car park [BE] parkeerplaats
car rental autoverhuurbedrijf
car seat kinderzitje
card kaart
careful voorzichtig
carpet tapijt
carry-on luggage handbagage
cart wagentje
carton doos
cash *adv* contant; *v* verzilveren
cash register kassa
casino casino
castle kasteel
catch pakken; **(bus)** nemen
cathedral kathedraal
caution oppassen
cave grot
CD cd
CD player cd-speler
cell phone (informal) mobiel;
(formal) mobiele telefoon
cemetery begraafplaats

ceramics keramiek
certificate certificaat
change (money) n wisselgeld;
  (buses) v overstappen; **(money)**
  v wisselen; **(reservation)**
  v veranderen; **(baby)** v verschonen
charcoal houtskool
charge n prijs; v berekenen
cheap goedkoop
check n rekening; v checken
check in inchecken
check out (hotel) uitchecken
checking account betaalrekening
cheers proost
chemical toilet chemisch toilet
chemist [BE] (with prescriptions)
  apotheek; **(without prescriptions)**
  drogisterij
cheque [BE] rekening
chest borstkas
child kind
child seat kinderstoeltje
child's cot [BE] wieg
children's clothing kinderkleding
children's menu kindermenu
children's portion kinderportie
choose selecteren
church kerk
cigarette sigaret
cigar sigaar
cinema [BE] bioscoop
class klas
clean schoon
cleaning supplies schoonmaakmiddelen
clearance opruiming
cliff klif
cling film [BE] huishoudfolie
clinic kliniek
clock klok

clog n klomp
close adv dichtbij; v sluiten
clothing store kledingwinkel
cloudy bewolkt
club club
coast kust
coat jas
coat check garderobe
coat hanger kleerhanger
code code
coin munt
cold (chilly) koud; **(flu)** verkoudheid
collapse instorten
colleague collega
collect ophalen
collection (mail) lichting
color kleur
comb kam
come komen
commission commissie
compact compact
company (business) bedrijf;
  (companionship) gezelschap
compartment (train) coupé
computer computer
concert concert
concert hall concertgebouw
concession concessie
concussion hersenschudding
conditioner conditioner
condom condoom
conductor dirigent
conference conferentie
confirm bevestigen
congratulations gefeliciteerd
connect verbinding maken
connection verbinding
conscious bewust
conservation area beschermd

display case vitrine
disposable wegwerpbaar
dissolve oplossen
distance afstand
disturb storen
dive duiken
diving equipment duikapparatuur
divorce scheiden
dizzy duizelig
do doen
dock dok
doctor dokter
dog hond
doll pop
dollar (U.S.) dollar
domestic binnenlands
donation gift
door deur
dosage dosering
double dubbel
double room tweepersoonskamer
downstairs beneden
downtown stadscentrum
dozen dozijn
dress *n* jurk; *v* aankleden
dress code kledingvoorschriften
drink *n* drankje; *v* drinken
drip druppelen
drive rijden
driver chauffeur
driver's license rijbewijs
drop (medicine) druppel
drown verdrinken
drowsy suf
drowsiness sufheid
drugstore drogisterij
drunk dronken
dry droog
dry clean stomen

dry cleaner stomerij
dubbed nagesynchroniseerd
dummy [BE] fopspeen
during tijdens
Dutch (language) Nederlands;
  (people) Nederlanders
duty (tax) accijns
duty-free belastingvrij

E

ear oor
ear drops oordruppels
earache oorpijn
early vroeg
earrings oorbellen
east oost
easy makkelijk
eat eten
economy class (general) economy
class; **(train)** tweede klas
electrical outlet stopcontact
electronic elektronisch
elevator *n* lift
e-mail e-mail
e-mail address e-mailadres
embassy ambassade
emerald smaragd
emergency noodgeval
emergency brake noodrem
emergency exit nooduitgang
emergency service hulpdienst
empty *adj* leeg; *v* leegmaken
end *n* einde; *v* aflopen
engaged (marriage) verloofd
England Engeland
English Engels
English-speaking Engelstalig
engrave graveren
enjoy leuk vinden
enlarge vergroten

enough genoeg
entertainment guide uitgids
entrance ingang
entrance fee toegangsprijs
entrance ramp (highway) oprit snelweg
entry ingang
entry visa inreisvisum
envelope envelop
epileptic epileptisch
equipment (clothing) uitrusting; **(machine)** apparatuur
error fout
escalator roltrap
essential essentieel
e-ticket e-ticket
euro euro
Eurocheque Eurocheque
evening avond
event evenement
every elk
exact exact
examination onderzoek
example voorbeeld
except uitgezonderd
excess luggage overbagage
exchange (general) ruilen; **(money)** wisselen
exchange rate wisselkoers
excursion excursie
exhausted uitgeput
exit (door) uitgang; **(highway)** afslag
exit ramp afrit
expensive duur
experience ervaring
expiration date vervaldatum
expose blootstellen
express mail per expres
extension (phone) toestel

extra (additional) extra
extract v onttrekken
eye oog
eyebrow wenkbrauw

F

fabric stof
face gezicht
facial n gezichtsbehandeling
facilities faciliteiten
factor factor
faint adj zwak; v flauwvallen
fall v vallen
family (immediate) gezin; **(relatives)** familie
famous beroemd
fan n ventilator
far ver
far-sighted verziend
farm boerderij
fast (speedy) snel; **(clock)** loopt voor
fast food fastfood
faucet kraan
faulty defect
favorite favoriet
fax fax
fax machine faxapparaat
fax number faxnummer
feature kenmerk
feed voeden
feel voelen
female vrouwelijk
ferry veerboot
fever koorts
few weinig
fiancé verloofde
field weiland
fight n gevecht; v vechten
fill vullen
fill out invullen

fill up opvullen
filling vulling
film (movie) film; **(camera)** fotorolletje
filter filter
find vinden
fine (good) goed; **(well)** prima; **(police)** boete
finger vinger
fire (campfire) kampvuur; **(disaster)** brand
fire alarm brandalarm
fire brigade [BE] brandweer
fire department brandweer
fire door branddeur
fire escape nooduitgang
fire exit brandtrap
fire extinguisher brandblusser
first eerst
first class eerste klas
fishing v vissen
fit passen
fitting room paskamer
fix (repair) repareren
flash flits
flashlight zaklantaarn
flavor smaak
flea market vlooienmarkt
flight vlucht
flight attendant (male) steward; (female) stewardess
flight number vluchtnummer
floor (level) verdieping
florist bloemenwinkel
flower bloem
flu griep
flush doorspoelen
fly n vlieg; v vliegen
fog mist
follow volgen

food voedsel
food poisoning voedselvergiftiging
foot voet
footpath [BE] voetpad
football [BE] voetbal
for voor
for sale te koop
foreign buitenlands
forest bos
forget vergeten
fork vork
form n formulier
formal dress avondkleding
formula (baby) flesvoeding
fountain fontein
fracture breuk
frame (glasses) montuur
free (available) vrij
free of charge gratis
freeze bevriezen
freezer diepvriezer
frequent adj vaak
fresh vers
friend vriend
from (general) van; **(destination)** uit
front voorkant
frying pan koekenpan
fuel (gas) benzine
full vol
fun plezier
funny grappig
furniture meubels
fuse zekering
fuse box zekeringkast

G

gallery galerie
game (competition) wedstrijd; **(tennis) game; (toy)** spelletje
garage garage

garbage bag vuilniszak
garden tuin
gas (gasoline) benzine
gas station benzinestation
gas tank benzinetank
gate (airport) gate; (general) hek
gauze gaas
gear versnelling
genuine echt
get (receive) krijgen
get off (bus) uitstappen
gift cadeau
gift store cadeauwinkel
girl meisje
girlfriend vriendin
give geven
glass (drinking) glas
glasses (optical) bril
gloves handschoenen
gluten gluten
go gaan
goggles duikbril
gold goud
golf golf
golf club golfstok
golf course golfbaan
good goed
goodbye dag
gram gram
grass gras
great prima
Great Britain Groot-Brittannië
green groen
greengrocer [BE] groenteman
groundcloth grondzeil
groundsheet [BE] grondzeil
group groep
guarantee garantie
guesthouse pension

guide (tour) gids
guide book gids
guide dog geleidehond
guided tour rondleiding
guided walk begeleide wandeling
guitar gitaar
gym fitnessruimte
gynecologist gynaecoloog

H

hair haar
hairbrush borstel
hairdresser dameskapper
halal halal
half n helft; adj halve
hammer hamer
hand hand
hand luggage handbagage
hand washable met de hand wassen
handbag [BE] handtas
handicapped gehandicapt
handicrafts ambachten
handkerchief zakdoek
hanger klerenhanger
hangover kater
happen gebeuren
happy blij
harbor haven
hard (tough) hard; (difficult) moeilijk
hardware store ijzerwarenwinkel
hat hoed
have hebben
hay fever hooikoorts
head hoofd
headache hoofdpijn
health gezondheid
health food reformproducten
health food store reformwinkel
health insurance
    ziektekostenverzekering

hear v horen
hearing aid gehoorapparaat
hearing impaired slechthorend
heart hart
heart attack hartaanval
heart condition hartkwaal
heat verwarming
heating [BE] verwarming
heavy zwaar
height (person) lengte;
  (general) hoogte
hello hallo
helmet helm
help helpen
her haar
here hier
hi hallo
high hoog
highchair kinderstoel
highway snelweg
hiking wandelen
hiking gear wandeluitrusting
hill heuvel
hire huren
historical historisch
hobby hobby
hold (general) vasthouden;
(phone) aan de lijn blijven
hole gat
holiday [BE] vakantie
home (place) thuis; **(direction)** naar
  huis
homemade zelfgemaakt
honeymoon huwelijksreis
horn claxon
horse paard
horseback riding paardrijden
horsetrack paardenrenbaan
hospital ziekenhuis

hot heet
hotel hotel
hour uur
house huis
how hoe
how much hoeveel
how many hoeveel
hug omhelzen
hunger honger
hungry hongerig
hunt jagen
hurry n haast; v haasten
hurt n pijn; v pijn hebben
husband man

I

I ik
ibuprofen ibuprofen
ice-cream parlor ijssalon
ice hockey ijshockey
ice skating schaatsen
identification legitimatiebewijs
ill [BE] ziek
illegal illegaal
imitation imitatie
important belangrijk
improve verbeteren
in in
incline helling
include bevatten
indigestion indigestie
indoor pool binnenbad
inexpensive goedkoop
infect ontsteken
infection infectie
inflammation ontsteking
informal informeel
information (general) informatie;
  (phone inquiry) inlichtingen
information desk informatiebalie

injection injectie
injure verwonden
innocent onschuldig
insect insect
insect bite insectenbeet
insect repellent insectenspray
insert (ATM) invoeren
inside binnen
insist aandringen
insomnia slapeloosheid
instant messenger instant messenger
instead of in plaats van
instructions gebruiksaanwijzing
instructor instructeur
insulin insuline
insurance verzekering
insurance card verzekeringsbewijs
insurance certificate [BE]
   verzekeringsbewijs
insurance claim schadeclaim
interest (hobby) interesse
interference storing
intermission pauze
international internationaal
International Student Card
Internationale Studentenkaart
internet internet
internet cafe internetcafé
internet service internetverbinding
interpreter tolk
intersection kruispunt
into naar
introduce (person) voorstellen
invite uitnodigen
iodine jodium
Ireland Ierland
iron n strijkijzer
is is
itch jeuk

item ding
itemized gespecificeerd

J

jacket jasje
jar pot
jaw kaak
jeans spijkerbroek
jet lag jetlag
jet-ski jetski
jeweler juwelier
jewelry sieraden
job baan
join meedoen
joint adj gezamenlijk; n gewricht
joke grap
journey reis

K

keep houden
keep out verboden toegang
key sleutel
key card sleutelkaart
key ring sleutelring
kiddie pool kinderbadje
kidney nier
kilo kilo
kilometer kilometer
kind (pleasant) aardig; **(type)** soort
kiss v kussen
kitchen keuken
knee knie
knife mes
knock kloppen
know kennen
kosher koosjer

L

label label
lace kant
lactose intolerant lactose-intolerant

ladder ladder
lake meer
lamp lamp
land *n* land; *v* landen
lane (traffic) rijstrook; **(path)** laantje
language course taalcursus
large groot
last (end) *adj* laatst; **(previous)** *adj* vorige; **(keep)** *v* meegaan
late (delayed) vertraagd
launderette [BE] wasserette
laundromat wasserette
laundry service wasserij
laundry facilities wasmachines
lawyer advocaat
laxative laxerend middel
lead (road) gaan naar
leader (group) groepsleider
leak lekken
learn leren
leather leer
leave (depart) vertrekken; **(deposit)** betalen; **(forget something)** vergeten
left links
left-luggage office [BE] bagagedepot
leg (body part) been
legal legaal
lend lenen
length lengte
lens lens
lens cap lensdop
less minder
lesson les
let laten
letter brief
level *adj* gelijk; *n* verdieping
library bibliotheek
life leven

life boat reddingsboot
life guard (pool) badmeester; **(beach)** strandmeester
life jacket reddingsvest
lift [BE] lift
light licht
lightbulb gloeilamp
lighthouse vuurtoren
lighter *adj* lichter; *n* aansteker
line lijn
linen linnen
lip lip
lipstick lippenstift
liquor store slijter
liter liter
little klein
live wonen
liver lever
living room woonkamer
loafers instappers
lobby (theater, hotel) hal
local plaatselijk
lock *n* slot; *v* afsluiten
log on inloggen
log off uitloggen
long lang
long-distance bus touringcar
long-sighted [BE] verziend
look *n* stijl; *v* kijken
loose los
lorry [BE] vrachtauto
lose verliezen
lost (misplaced) verloren; **(direction)** verdwaald
lost-and-found gevonden voorwerpen
lost property office [BE] gevonden voorwerpen
lottery loterij
loud (general) luid; **(voice)** hard

love *n* liefde; **(general)** *v* dol zijn op;
  (romantic) *v* houden van
low laag
luggage bagage
luggage cart bagagewagentje
luggage trolley [BE] bagagewagentje
lump gezwel
lunch lunch
lung long

M

machine washable in de machine
  wassen
madam mevrouw
magazine tijdschrift
magnificent magnifiek
mail *n* post; *v* posten
mailbox brievenbus
main grootste
make-up make-up
male mannelijk
mall winkelcentrum
mallet houten hamer
man man
manager manager
mandatory verplicht
manicure manicure
many veel
map kaart
market markt
marry trouwen
mascara mascara
mask masker
mass mis
massage massage
matches lucifers
matinee matinee
mattress matras
maybe misschien
meal maaltijd

mean *v* betekenen
measure meten
measurement afmeting
measuring cup maatbeker
measuring spoon maatlepel
mechanic monteur
medication medicijn
medicine geneesmiddel
meet ontmoeten
meeting vergadering
meeting room vergaderruimte
meeting place ontmoetingsplaats
member lid
memorial gedenkteken
memory card geheugenkaart
mend (clothes) verstellen
menstrual cramps menstruatiepijn
menu menukaart
merge (traffic) invoegen
message bericht
metal metaal
microwave (oven) magnetron
midday [BE] twaalf uur 's middags
midnight middernacht
migraine migraine
mini-bar minibar
minute minuut
mirror spiegel
missing kwijt
mistake fout
mobile home camper
mobile phone [BE] (informal) mobiel;
  (formal) mobiele telefoon
moisturizer (cream)
vochtinbrengende crème
money geld
money order postwissel
month maand
mop dweil

moped brommer
more meer
morning ochtend
mosque moskee
mosquito bite muggenbeet
motion sickness reisziekte
motor motor
motor boat motorboot
motorcycle motorfiets
motorway [BE] snelweg
mountain berg
mountain bike mountainbike
moustache snor
mouth mond
move (general) bewegen;
 (relocate) verhuizen
movie film
movie theater bioscoop
Mr. De heer (Dhr.); meneer
Mrs. Mevrouw (Mevr.)
much veel
mugging beroving
mug mok
muscle spier
museum museum
music muziek
must moeten

N

nail nagel
nail file nagelvijl
nail salon nagelsalon
name naam
napkin servet
nappy [BE] luier
narrow smal
national nationaal
nationality nationaliteit
native inwoner
nature natuur

nature reserve natuurreservaat
nature trail natuurpad
nausea misselijkheid
nauseous misselijk
near dichtbij
nearby in de buurt
nearest dichtstbijzijnde
near-sighted bijziend
necessary nodig
neck nek
necklace halsketting
need v nodig hebben
network netwerk
never nooit
new nieuw
New Zealand Nieuw-Zeeland
news nieuws
news agent [BE] kiosk
newspaper krant
newsstand kiosk
next volgende
next to naast
nice fijn
night nacht
night club nachtclub
no (denial) nee; **(prohibition)** niet
no parking parkeerverbod
noisy lawaaierig
non-EU citizens niet-EU-ingezetenen
non-smoking niet-roken
non-stop non-stop
noon twaalf uur 's middags
normal normaal
north noord
nose neus
not niet
nothing niets
notify informeren
now nu

number nummer
nurse verpleegster
nylon nylon

O

o'clock uur
office kantoor
office hours kantooruren
office supplies
    kantoorbenodigdheden
off-licence [BE] slijter
off-peak (ticket) daluren
office kantoor
often vaak
oil olie
OK oké
old oud
on op
once één keer
one-way (traffic)
    eenrichtingsverkeer
one-way ticket enkeltje
only slechts
open adj open; (shop)
    v opengaan; **(window)** v opendoen
opening hours [BE] openingstijden
opera opera
operation operatie
opposite tegenover
opticien opticiën
or of
orally oraal
orchestra orkest
order bestellen
organize organiseren
original origineel
out uit
outdoor adj openlucht
outdoor pool buitenbad
outside buiten

oval ovaal
oven oven
over (more than) meer dan
overcharged teveel betaald
overheat oververhit worden
overlook uitkijkpunt
overnight in één nacht
owe verschuldigd zijn
own adj eigen; v bezitten
owner eigenaar
oxygen zuurstof

P

pacifier fopspeen
pack inpakken
package pakje
paddling pool [BE] kinderzwembad
padlock hangslot
pail emmer
pain pijn
paint v verven
painting schilderij
pair paar
pajamas pyjama
palace paleis
palpitations hartkloppingen
panorama panorama
pants lange broek
panty hose panty
paper towel keukenpapier
paracetamol [BE] paracetamol
paralysis verlamming
parcel [BE] pak
parents ouders
park n park; v parkeren
parking garage parkeergarage
parking lot parkeerplaats
parking meter parkeermeter
parking ticket parkeerbon
partner partner

part time parttime
party (social) feestje
pass (a place) langskomen;
(traffic) inhalen
passenger passagier
passport paspoort
password wachtwoord
pastry store banketbakker
patient *adj* geduldig; *n* patiënt
pavement [BE] stoep
pay phone telefoonzuil
pay betalen
payment betaling
pearl parel
pedestrian voetganger
pedestrian crossing
    voetgangersoversteekplaats
pedestrian zone verkeersvrij gebied
pediatrician kinderarts
pedicure pedicure
peg wasknijper
pen pen
penicillin penicilline
per per
performance voorstelling
perhaps misschien
period (general) periode;
    (menstrual) menstruatie
person persoon
petite tenger
petrol [BE] benzine
petrol station [BE] benzinestation
pewter tin
pharmacy apotheek
phone *n* telefoon; *v* telefoneren
phone call telefoongesprek
phone card telefoonkaart
phone directory telefoongids
phone number telefoonnummer

photocopy n kopie; v kopiëren
photograph foto
photography fotografie
phrase zinsnede
phrase book taalgids
pick up *v* ophalen
picnic picknick
picnic area picknickplaats
piece stuk
pill pil
pillow kussen
PIN PIN
pipe (smoking) pijp
pizzeria pizzeria
place plaats
plane vliegtuig
plan plan
plaster [BE] pleister
plastic plastic
plastic wrap huishoudfolie
plate bord
platform spoor
platinum platina
play *n* toneelstuk; *v* spelen
playground speeltuin
playpen babybox
pleasant prettig
please alstublieft
plug plug
plunger ontstopper
pneumonia longontsteking
poison gif
police politie
police report proces-verbaal
police station politiebureau
pollen count stuifmeelgehalte
polyester polyester
pond vijver
pool zwembad

popular populair
porcelain porselein
port (harbor) haven
porter kruier
portion portie
post [BE] *n* post; *v* versturen
post office postkantoor
postage posttarief
postbox [BE] brievenbus
postcard ansichtkaart
pot pot
pottery aardewerk
pound pond
pound sterling Britse pond
power (electricity) stroom
practice praktijk
pregnant zwanger
premium (gas) super
prepaid phone card prepaidkaart
prescription recept
present *n* cadeau; *v* geven
press persen
pretty mooi
price prijs
print afdrukken
prison gevangenis
private particulier
produce store groentewinkel
profession beroep
problem probleem
prohibited verboden
program programma
pronounce uitspreken
pub pub
public *n* publiek; *adj* openbaar
pull trekken
pump pomp
pure zuiver
purpose doel

purse (handbag) handtas
push duwen
pushchair [BE] kinderwagen
put neerzetten

Q

quality kwaliteit
quarter kwart
queue [BE] *n* rij; *v* in de rij staan
quick snel
quiet rustig

R

racetrack circuit
racket (tennis) racket
railroad crossing overweg
railway station [BE] station
rain *n* regen; *v* regenen
raincoat regenjas
rape verkrachting
rapids stroomversnelling
rash uitslag
razor scheerapparaat
reach bereiken
reaction reactie
read lezen
ready klaar
real (genuine) echt
receipt (in shop) bon;
  (formal) kwitantie
receive ontvangen
reception (desk) receptie
receptionist receptionist
recommend aanbevelen
reduce verminderen
reduction korting
refrigerator koelkast
refund *n* terugbetaling;
  v terugbetalen
region streek
registered mail aangetekende post

registration form inschrijfformulier
regular normaal
relationship relatie
reliable betrouwbaar
religion godsdienst
remember (recall) herinneren;
(not forget) onthouden
remove verwijderen
renovation renovatie
rent *n* huur; *v* huren
rental car huurauto
repair repareren
repeat herhalen
replace vervangen
replacement part
vervangingsonderdeel
report *n* rapport; *v* melden
required vereist
reservation reservering
reservation desk reserveringsbalie
reserve reserveren
reservoir reservoir
responsibility verantwoordelijkheid
rest rusten
rest area rustgebied
restaurant restaurant
restroom toilet
retired gepensioneerd
return ticket [BE] retourtje
right (correct) juist; **(direction)** rechts
ring ring
river rivier
road weg
road map wegenkaart
roadwork wegwerkzaamheden
rob beroven
robbery beroving
rock rots
romantic romantisch

roof dak
room kamer
room service roomservice
rope touw
rose roos
round rond
round-trip ticket retourtje
route route
row roeien
rowboat roeiboot
rubbish [BE] vuilnis
rude onbeleefd
ruins ruïne
rush haasten

S

safe *adj* veilig; *n* kluis
safety veiligheid
safety pin veiligheidsspeld
sale opruiming
sales tax BTW
same hetzelfde
sand zand
sandals sandalen
sanitary napkin maandverband
sanitary pad [BE] maandverband
satin satijn
saucepan steelpan
sauna sauna
save (computer) opslaan
savings account spaarrekening
say zeggen
scarf sjaal
scissors schaar
Scotland Schotland
screwdriver schroevendraaier
sea zee
seasick zeeziek
season ticket abonnement
seat (on train, etc.) plaats

seat belt veiligheidsgordel
sedative kalmerend middel
see zien
self-service zelfbediening
sell verkopen
seminar seminar
send versturen
senior citizen oudere
separated uit elkaar
separate apart
serious ernstig
serve opdienen
service (church) kerkdienst;
   (restaurant) bediening
service charge bedieningsgeld
service included bediening inbegrepen
set menu dagmenu
sew naaien
sex seks
shadow schaduw
shallow ondiep
shampoo shampoo
shape vorm
share delen
sharp scherp
shave scheren
shaving brush scheerkwast
shaving cream scheerzeep
sheet (bed) laken
ship schip
shirt (men's) overhemd
shock schok
shoe schoen
shoe repair schoenmaker
shoe store schoenenwinkel
shop assistant winkelbediende
shopping n boodschappen;
   v winkelen
shopping basket winkelmandje

shopping centre [BE] winkelcentrum
shopping mall winkelcentrum
shopping cart winkelwagentje
shopping trolley [BE] winkelwagentje
short kort
short-sighted [BE] bijziend
shorts korte broek
shoulder schouder
shovel schep
show tonen
shower douche
shut v sluiten
shutter luik
sick (general) ziek; (nauseous) misselijk
side effect bijwerking
sidewalk stoep
sight (attraction)
   bezienswaardigheid
sightseeing tour toeristische rondrit
sign (road) n verkeersbord;
   (place signature) v tekenen
silk zijde
silver zilver
single (person) single
single ticket [BE] (travel) enkeltje
single room eenpersoonskamer
sink (bathroom) wastafel;
   (kitchen) gootsteen
sit zitten
site plaats
size maat
skating rink ijsbaan
skin huid
skirt rok
sleep slapen
sleeping bag slaapzak
sleeping car slaapwagen
sleeping pill slaappil
sleeve mouw

slice plak
slippers pantoffels
slow langzaam
small klein
smell geur
smoke roken
smoking area rokerszone
snack snack
snack bar snackbar
sneakers gymschoenen
snorkle snorkelen
snow n sneeuw; v sneeuwen
soap zeep
soccer voetbal
socket stopcontact
socks sokken
sold out uitverkocht
some enkele
someone iemand
something iets
sometimes soms
somewhere ergens
soon gauw
soother [BE] fopspeen
sore pijnlijk
sore throat keelpijn
sorry sorry
south zuid
souvenir souvenir
souvenir guide souvenirgids
souvenir store souvenirwinkel
spa kuuroord
space ruimte
spare extra
spatula spatel
speak spreken
special speciaal
specialist specialist
specimen monster

speed snelheid
speed limit snelheidslimiet
spell v spellen
spend uitgeven
sponge spons
spoon lepel
sport sport
sporting goods store sportwinkel
sports club sportvereniging
spot (place, site) plaats
spouse (male) echtgenoot;
　(female) echtgenote
sprain n verstuiking; v verstuiken
square vierkant
stadium stadion
staff personeel
stainless steel roestvrij staal
stairs trap
stamp n postzegel; v stempelen
stand staan
standard standaard
standby ticket standby-ticket
start (general) beginnen;
　(car, etc.) starten
statue standbeeld
stay n verblijf; **(remain)** v blijven;
　(overnight) v logeren
steal stelen
steel staal
steep steil
sterilizing solution steriele oplossing
sterling silver sterling zilver
stiff stijf
still nog
stolen gestolen
stomach maag
stomachache maagpijn
stop n halte; v stoppen
store winkel

store directory [BE] winkelplattegrond
store guide winkelplattegrond
stove fornuis
straight recht
stream beekje
street straat
stroller kinderwagen
strong sterk
student student
study studeren
stunning verbluffend
style *n* stijl; *v* stylen
subtitled ondertiteld
suburb buitenwijk
subway metro
subway map metrokaart
subway station metrostation
suggest voorstellen
suit pak
suitable geschikt
suitcase koffer
sun zon
sunbathe zonnebaden
sunblock sunblock
sunburn zonnebrand
sunglasses zonnebril
sunshade [BE] parasol
sunscreen zonnebrandcrème
suntan lotion zonnebrandcrème
super (petrol) [BE] super
superb voortreffelijk
supermarket supermarkt
supervision toezicht
suppository zetpil
surcharge toeslag
sure zeker
surfboard surfplank
swallow doorslikken
sweater trui

sweatshirt sweatshirt
sweep vegen
sweet zoet
swelling zwelling
swim zwemmen
swimsuit zwempak
swimming pool zwembad
swimming trunks zwembroek
swollen opgezet
symbol symbool
symptom symptoom
synagogue synagoge
synthetic synthetisch

T
T-shirt T-shirt
TV tv
table tafel
tablet tablet
take (general) nemen;
  (carry) meenemen;
  (medicine) innemen; **(time)** duren
take off (plane) opstijgen;
  (shoes) uitdoen
talk praten
tall lang
tampon tampon
tap [BE] kraan
taste **n** smaak; **v** proeven
taxi taxi
taxi rank [BE] taxistandplaats
taxi stand taxistandplaats
teaspoon theelepel
team team
tear (muscle) scheuren
tear off afscheuren
telephone *n* telefoon; *v* telefoneren
telephone booth telefoonzuil
telephone call telefoongesprek
telephone number telefoonnummer

tell vertellen
temperature temperatuur
tennis tennis
tennis court tennisbaan
tent tent
tent peg tentharing
tent pole tentstok
terminal terminal
terrible vreselijk
text *n* tekst
text messaging sms'en
thank danken
that dat
theater theater
theft diefstal
then (time) dan
there daar
thermometer thermometer
thermos thermosfles
these deze
thick dik
thief dief
thigh dij
thin dun
thing ding
think denken
thirsty dorstig
this dit
those die
throat keel
through door
thumb duim
ticket kaartje
ticket inspector conducteur
ticket office loket
tie *n* stropdas
tight krap
tile tegel
time tijd

timetable [BE] dienstregeling
tip fooi
tire band
tired moe
tissue tissue
to (place) naar
tobacco tabak
tobacconist sigarenwinkel
today vandaag
toe teen
toilet [BE] toilet
toilet paper toiletpapier
toll tol
toll booth tolhuisje
toll road tolweg
tomorrow morgen
tongue tong
tonight vanavond
too te
tooth tand
toothache kiespijn
toothbrush tandenborstel
toothpaste tandpasta
top bovenkant
torn gescheurd
tour excursie
tour guide reisgids
tourist toerist
tourist office VVV-kantoor
tournament toernooi
tow truck takelwagen
towel handdoek
tower toren
town stad
town hall stadhuis
town map stadsplattegrond
town square stadsplein
toy speelgoed
toy store speelgoedwinkel

traditional traditioneel
traffic verkeer
traffic circle rotonde
traffic jam file
traffic light stoplicht
traffic offence [BE]
    verkeersovertreding
traffic violation verkeersovertreding
trail wandelpad
trailer aanhangwagen
train trein
train station station
tram tram
transfer overstappen
transport vervoer
translate vertalen
translation vertaling
translator vertaler
trash vuilnis
trash can vuilnisbak
travel reizen
travel agency reisbureau
travel sickness reisziekte
traveler's check reischeque
traveller's cheque [BE] reischeque
tray plateau
treatment behandeling
tree boom
trim bijknippen
trip reis
trolley wagentje
trousers [BE] lange broek
truck vrachtwagen
true waar
try on (clothes) passen
tumor tumor
tunnel tunnel
turn (traffic) keren
turn down (volume, heat) lager
    zetten
turn off uitzetten
turn on aanzetten
turn up hoger zetten
tweezers pincet
twist (ankle) verstuiken
typical typisch

U

U.K. Groot-Brittannië
U.S. Verenigde Staten
ugly lelijk
ulcer zweer
umbrella paraplu
unconscious bewusteloos
under onder
underground station
    [BE] metrostation
understand begrijpen
unemployed werkeloos
units (phone card) eenheden
until tot
upstairs boven
urgent dringend
use *n* gebruik; *v* gebruiken
username gebruikersnaam

V

vacant vrij
vacation vakantie
vacuum cleaner stofzuiger
valet service parkeerdienst
valid geldig
validate (general) bevestigen;
    (ticket) afstempelen
valuable waardevol
value waarde
VAT [BE] BTW
vegan veganist
vegetarian *n* vegetariër; *adj*
    vegetarisch

vehicle voertuig
vein ader
version versie
very heel
video game videospelletje
view uitzicht
viewpoint uitkijkpunt
village dorp
vineyard wijngaard
visa visum
visit *n* bezoek; *v* bezoeken
visiting hours bezoekuur
visually impaired slechtziend
volleyball volleybal
voltage voltage
vomit *n* braaksel; *v* overgeven

W

wait wachten
waiting room wachtkamer
waiter kelner
waitress kelnerin
wake (self) wakker worden;
  (someone) wakker maken
wake-up service wekdienst
Wales Wales
walk (general) lopen;
(on trail/path) wandelen
wall muur
wallet portemonnee
ward (hospital) afdeling
warm *adj* warm; *v* opwarmen
war memorial oorlogsmonument
warning waarschuwing
washable wasbaar
washing machine wasmachine
watch (timepiece) horloge
water water
water skis waterski's
waterfall waterval

waterproof waterdicht
wave golf
way weg
wear dragen
weather weer
weather forecast weerbericht
wedding huwelijk
week week
weekday weekdag
weekend weekend
weekend rate weekendtarief
weekly wekelijks
weigh wegen
weight gewicht
welcome welkom
west west
wetsuit duikerspak
what wat
wheelchair rolstoel
wheelchair ramp rolstoelopgang
when wanneer
where waar
which welke
while terwijl
who wie
whose van wie
why waarom
wide breed
wife vrouw
wildlife dieren in het wild
wind wind
windbreaker windjack
windmill molen
windscreen voorruit
windsurfing windsurfen
windy winderig
window (general) raam;
  (shop) etalage
window seat plaats bij het raam

wine wijn
wine list wijnkaart
wipe vegen
wireless draadloos
wish wens
with met
withdraw (money) opnemen
withdrawal (money) geldopname
within (time) binnen
without zonder
witness getuige
wood (forest) bos; **(material)** hout
wool wol
work (function) n werk
   v werken; **(operate)** bedienen
wrap v inpakken
write schrijven
wrong verkeerd

X

x-ray röntgenfoto

Y

yacht jacht
year jaar
yes ja
yesterday gisteren
yield (traffic) voorrang verlenen
you (sing. for.) u; (sing. inf.) jij;
   (pl. for.) u; (pl. inf.) jullie
young jong
youth jongeren
youth hostel jeugdherberg

Z

zebra crossing [BE] zebrapad
zero nul
zipper ritssluiting
zoo dierentuin

Dutch – English

A

aanbevelen recommend
aandringen insist
aangetekend registered (mail)
aangeven declare
aankleden v dress
aankomst arrivals
aansteker n lighter
aantrekkelijk attractive
aanvaarden accept
aanval attack
aanvang start
aanwijzen indicate
aanwijzingen directions (map)
aanzetten turn on
aardewerk pottery

aardig pleasant
accepteren accept
accijns duty
accu battery
achter behind
achterkant back (opposite of front)
acupunctuur acupuncture
adapter adapter
ademhalen breathe
ader vein
adres address
advocaat lawyer
afdeling department (general);
   ward (hospital)
afdrukken print
afhalen to go (food) [take away BE]

afleveren deliver (bring)
aflopen v end
afmeting measurement
afrit exit ramp
afschuwelijk awful
afslag highway [motorway BE] exit
afsluiten v lock
afspraak appointment
afstand distance
afstempelen validate
aftershave aftershave
afval trash [rubbish BE]
afwasmachine dishwasher
airco air conditioning
akkoord gaan agree
al already
alle all
alleen only (merely); alone
  (without company)
allergie allergy
allergisch allergic
alstublieft (a.u.b.) please
alternatief alternative
altijd always
aluminiumfolie aluminum
  [kitchen BE] foil
ambachten handicrafts
ambassade embassy
ambassadeur ambassador
ambulance ambulance
Amerikaan n American
Amerikaans adj American
andere other
annuleren cancel
ansichtkaart post card
antacidum antacid
antibiotica antibiotics
antiek antique
antiseptisch adj antiseptic

antivries antifreeze
annuleren cancel
apart separate
apparatuur equipment
appartement apartment
apotheek pharmacy [chemist BE]
arm arm
armband bracelet
aromatherapie aromatherapy
arriveren arrive
artritis arthritis
asbak ashtray
aspirine aspirin
assistentie assistance
astma asthma
atletiek athletics
audiogids audio guide
Australië Australia
authentiek authentic
auto car
autodek car deck (ferry)
autosnelweg highway
[motorway BE]
autoverhuur car rental [car hire BE]
avond evening
avondeten dinner
avondkleding formal wear

B

baan job
baby baby
babybox playpen
babydoekjes baby wipes
babyvoeding baby food
bad bath
badkamer bathroom
badmeester life guard (pool)
bagageafhaalruimte baggage claim
bagage luggage [baggage BE]
bagagedepot luggage

[baggage BE] check
bagagekluisjes luggage lockers
bagagewagentje luggage cart
[baggage trolley BE]
bakkerij bakery
bal ball
balkon balcony
ballet ballet
band band
bank bank
banketbakker pastry shop
bar bar
basketbal basketball
batterij battery
bed bed
beddengoed bedding
bedienen work (operate)
bediening service
bediening inbegrepen service included
bedieningsgeld service charge
bedrag amount
bedrijf company (business)
bedrijvencomplex business center
beekje stream
been leg
beet bite
beginnen v begin
beginner beginner
begraafplaats cemetery
begrijpen understand
beha bra
behalve except
behandeling treatment
belangrijk important
belastingvrij duty free
België Belgium
bellen call
benzine gas [petrol BE]
benzinestation gas [petrol BE] station
benzinetank gas tank

bereiken reach
berg mountain
bericht message
beroemd famous
beroep profession
beroven rob
beschikbaar available
beschrijven describe
besmettelijk contagious
bestellen v order
bestemming destination
bestuurder driver
betalen pay
betaling payment
betekenen v mean
betrouwbaar reliable
bevatten contain
bevestigen confirm
bevriezen freeze
bevroren frozen
bewaren keep
bewegen move
bewust conscious
bewusteloos unconscious
bezem broom
bezet taken
bezienswaardigheid sight
(attraction)
bezitten v own
bezoek n visit
bezoeken v visit
bezoekuur visiting hours
bibliotheek library
bijgewerkt updated
bijknippen v trim
bijna almost
bijten bite
bijziend near-sighted
[short-sighted BE]
bikini bikini

binnen inside
binnenbad indoor pool
binnenkomen enter
binnenkomst entrance
binnenlands domestic
bioscoop movie theater [cinema BE]
bitter bitter
bizar bizarre
blaar blister
blaas bladder
bladeren browse
blauwe plek bruise
bleekmiddel bleach
blij happy
blijven stay
blikopener can opener
blind blind
blindedarm appendix
bloed blood
bloedarmoede anemia
bloeddruk blood pressure
bloedgroep blood group
bloeden bleed
bloem flower
bloemenwinkel flower shop
bloemist florist
bloes blouse
blokkeren v block
blootstellen expose
boarden boarding (airport)
boardingkaart boarding card
bocht curve
boek book
boekwinkel bookstore
boerderij farm
boete fine (police)
boksen boxing
bon receipt
boodschappen n shopping
boom tree

boottocht boat trip
bord plate
borgsom deposit
borst breast
borst geven breastfeed
borstel hairbrush
borstkas chest
bos forest
bot bone
botanische tuin botanical garden
bouwen build
boven above
bovenkant top
braaksel n vomit
brand n fire
brandalarm fire alarm
brandblusser fire extinguisher
branddeur fire door
brandstof fuel
brandtrap fire exit
brandweer fire department [brigade BE]
brandweerkazerne fire station
brandwond burn
breed wide
breken v break
breuk fracture
brief letter
brievenbus mailbox [postbox BE]
bril glasses (optical)
Brit n British
Brits adj British
Britse pond pound sterling
broche brooch
brochure brochure
broer brother
brommer moped
brug bridge
bruin brown
bruinen v tan

buiten outside
buitenbad outdoor pool
buitenlands foreign
buitenlijn outside line (phone)
buiten werking out of order
buitenwijk suburb
bus bus
busbaan bus lane
bushalte bus stop
bushokje bus shelter
business class businessclass
busroute bus route
busstation bus station
butagas butane gas

C

cadeau gift
cadeauwinkel gift store
café cafe
calorie calorie
camper mobile home
camping campsite
Canada Canada
capsule capsule (medication)
casino casino
cd CD
cd-speler CD player
certificaat certificate
chauffeur driver
check-in balie check-in desk (airport)
chemisch toilet chemical toilet
circuit racetrack
claxon horn
club club
code code
collect call collect call
[reversed charges BE]
collega colleague
commissie commission
compact compact

computer computer
concert concert
concertgebouw concert hall
concessie concession
conciërge concierge
conditioner conditioner
condoom condom
conducteur ticket inspector
conferentie conference
conferentiezaal conference room
congres convention
congresgebouw convention hall
constant constant
constipatie constipation
consulaat consulate
contactlens contact lens
contactlensvloeistof contact lens
  solution
contant cash
controle n control
cosmetisch cosmetic
coupé compartment (train)
couvert cover charge
creditcard credit card
cruise n cruise
cruisen v cruise

D

daar there
dag day (time period); hello; goodbye
dagelijks daily
dak roof
dames women's restroom
dameskapper hairdresser
dameskleding ladieswear
dan then (time)
danken thank
dans n dance
dansen v dance
dat that

decoratief decorative
defect faulty
deken blanket
delen v share
Delfts blauw Delft blue
delicatessen delicatessen
denken think
deodorant deodorant
deposito deposit
detail detail
deur door
De heer (Dhr.) Mr.
de weg wijzen v direct
diamant diamond
diarree diarrhea
dichtbij near
dieet diet
dief thief
diefstal theft
dienblad tray
dienst n service
diep deep
diepvriezer freezer
dier animal
dierentuin zoo
diesel diesel
digitaal digital
dij thigh
dik thick
dineren dine
ding thing
directeur director
dirigent conductor
discotheek dance club
discountzaak discount store
dobbelsteen dice
doel purpose
dok dock
dokter doctor

donker dark
doodlopende weg dead end
doof deaf
dood dead
door through (movement);
    by (by means of)
doorgaand verkeer through traffic
doorlopend continuous
doorslikken swallow
doorspoelen v flush
doos box
dorp village
dorstig thirsty
dosering dosage
douane customs
douaneaangifteformulier
customs declaration form
douanecontrole customs control
douche shower
dozijn dozen
draadloos wireless
draaien v turn (general); play (movie)
dragen wear (clothes)
drankje n drink
dringend urgent
drinken v drink
drogist drugstore [chemist BE]
dronken drunk
droog dry
druk busy
drukken press (clothing)
druppel drop (medication)
druppelen drip
duikbril goggles
duiken v dive
duikerspak wetsuit
duim thumb
duizelig dizzy
dun thin

duren _v_ take (time)
duur expensive
duwen push
dweil mop

E

echt real
echtgenoot spouse (male)
echtgenote spouse (female)
echtheid authenticity
eenheden units (phone card)
eenpersoonskamer single room
eenrichtingsstraat one-way street
eenrichtingsverkeer one-way (traffic)
eerst first
eerste klas first class
eerstehulp (EHBO) first aid
eetkamer dining room
eetlust appetite
eigen _adj_ own
eigendom property
einde _n_ end
elektrisch electric
elektronisch electronic
elk every
e-mail e-mail
e-mailadres e-mail address
en and
Engeland England
Engels English
enkeltje one-way [single BE] ticket
envelop envelope
epileptisch epileptic
ergens somewhere
ernstig serious
ervaring experience
essentieel essential
eten eat
e-ticket e-ticket
euro euro

Eurocheque Eurocheque
even briefly
evenement event
exact exact
excursie tour
expres express
extra adj additional

F

faciliteiten facilities
factor factor
familie family
fastfood fast food
favoriet favorite
fax fax
faxapparaat fax machine
faxnummer fax number
feestdag holiday
feestje party (social)
fiets bicycle
fietspad bicycle path
fietsen cycling
fietsroute bicycle route
fijn nice
file traffic jam
film film (camera); movie [film BE]
filter filter
fitnessruimte gym
flat apartment [flat BE]
flauwvallen _v_ faint
fles bottle
flesopener bottle opener
flesvoeding formula (baby)
flits flash
floss dental floss
föhn hair dryer
fontein fountain
fooi tip
fopspeen pacifier [soother BE]
formulier form

fornuis stove
foto photograph
fotografie photography
fotorolletje film
fototoestel camera
fout mistake

G

gaan go
gaas gauze
galerie gallery
gang hallway (building); course (meal)
gangpad aisle
garage garage
garantie guarantee
garderobe coat check
gat hole
gate gate (airport)
gauw soon
gay club gay club
gebeuren happen
geboortedatum date of birth
geboren born
gebouw building
gebroken broken
gebruik n use
gebruiken v use
gebruikersnaam username
gebruiksaanwijzing instructions
gedenkteken memorial
geduldig adj patient
geel yellow
geen no
gefeliciteerd congratulations
gehandicapt disabled
geheugenkaart memory card
gehoorapparaat hearing aid
gekoeld refrigerated
geld money
geldig valid

geldautomaat ATM
geldopname withdrawal (money)
geldwisselkantoor currency exchange
geleden ago
geleidehond guide dog
gelijk adv level
gelukkig fortunately
genoeg enough
geopend open
gepensioneerd retired
geschenk gift
geschikt voor de magnetron
    microwaveable
geschikt suitable
getuige witness
geur smell
gevaarlijk dangerous
gevecht n fight
geven give
gevonden voorwerpen lost and found
    [lost property office BE]
gevorderd advanced
gewicht weight
gewricht n joint
gezelschap company
    (companionship)
gezicht face
gezichtsbehandeling n facial
gezin family (immediate)
gezondheid health
gezwel lump
gids guide (tour, book)
gif poison
gift donation
gisteren yesterday
gitaar guitar
glad icy
glas glass (drinking)
gloeilamp light bulb

gluten gluten
godsdienst religion
goed adj good
goederen freight
goedkeuren approve
goedkoop cheap
golf golf (game); wave (water)
golfbaan golf course
golfstok golf club
gootsteen sink
gordijn curtain
goud gold
graad degree
gracht canal
gram gram
grap joke
grappig funny
gras grass
grasduinen browse
gratis free of charge
graveren engrave
griep flu
groentewinkel produce store
    [greengrocer BE]
groep group
grondzeil groundcloth
    [groundsheet BE]
groot large
Groot-Brittannië Great Britain
grot cave
gymschoenen sneakers
gynaecoloog gynecologist

H

haar hair
haarspray hairspray
haast n rush
haasten v rush
hal hall (general); lobby (theater, hotel)
halal halal

hallo hello
half half
halsketting necklace
halte stop (bus, tram)
hamer hammer
hand hand
handbagage carry-on [hand BE] luggage
handdoek towel
handschoenen gloves
handtas purse [handbag BE]
handwerkwinkel craft shop
hangslot padlock
hard hard
hart heart
hartaanval heart attack
hartkloppingen palpitations
hartkwaal heart condition
haven harbor
hebben have
heel very
heerlijk lovely
heet hot
hek gate
helft n half
helling incline
helm helmet
helpen help
herenkapper barber
herenkleding menswear
herentoilet men's restroom
herhalen repeat
herinneren remember
hersenschudding concussion
hetzelfde same
heuvel hill
hier here
hij he
historisch historical
hobby hobby

hoe how
hoed hat
hoek corner
hoest *n* cough
hoesten *v* cough
hoeveel how much; how many
hoeveelheid amount
hoger zetten turn up
hond dog
honger hunger
hongerig hungry
honkbal baseball
hoofd head
hoofdpijn headache
hoofdweg main road
hoogte height
hooikoorts hay fever
horen hear
horloge watch
hotel hotel
houden keep
houden van *v* love
hout wood
houten hamer mallet
houtskool charcoal
huid skin
huis house
huishoudfolie plastic wrap
  [cling film BE]
hulp assistance
hulpdienst emergency service
huren rent
hut cabin
huurauto rental car
huwelijk wedding
huwelijksreis honeymoon

I

iemand someone
Ierland Ireland

iets something
ijsbaan skating rink
ijssalon ice-cream parlor
ijshockey ice hockey
ijzerwarenwinkel hardware store
ik I
illegaal illegal
imitatie imitation
in in
inbegrepen included (price)
ibuprofen ibuprofen
incheckbalie check-in desk
inchecken check-in
indigestie indigestion
infectie infection
informeel informal
informeren notify
informatie information
informatiebalie information desk
informatiebureau information office
ingang entrance
inhalen *v* pass
inhaalverbod no-passing zone
injectie injection
inloggen log on
innemen take (medication)
inpakken pack (suitcase); wrap
  (present)
inreisvisum entry visa
inrijden enter (traffic)
insectenbeet insect bite
insectenspray insect repellent
inslaan break
instant messenger
  instant messenger
instappers loafers
instorten collapse
instructeur instructor
insuline insulin

intensive care intensive care
interessant interesting
interesse interest (hobby)
internationaal international
Internationale Studentenkaart
    International Student Card
internet internet
internetcafé internet cafe
internetverbinding internet service
intoetsen enter
invullen fill out
invoegen merge (traffic)
invoeren insert
inwendig internally
inwerpen insert
inwoner resident
inwoners van de EU EU citizens

J

ja yes
jaar year
jaar oud aged
jacht yacht
jagen hunt
jas coat
jasje jacket
jazz jazz
jetlag jet lag
jetski jet-ski
jeugdherberg youth hostel
jeuk n itch
jij you (informal)
jodium iodine
jong young
jongen boy
jongeren youth
juist correct
jurk n dress
juwelier jeweler

K

kaak jaw
kaars candle
kaart card (credit card); map
    (directions)
kaartje ticket
kakkerlak cockroach
kalender calendar
kalmerend middel sedative
kam comb
kamer room
kamermeisje maid (hotel)
kamertarief room rate
kamperen v camp
kampvuur fire
kan jug
kanaal canal
kanker cancer
kanovaren canoeing
kant lace
kantoor office
kantoorbenodigdheden
    office supplies
kapot broken
kapper barber; hairdresser
kapsel hair cut
karaf carafe
kassa checkout; cash register
kassajuffrouw cashier
kasteel castle
kater hangover
kathedraal cathedral
keel throat
katoen cotton
keelpijn sore throat
keer time
kelder basement
kelner waiter
kelnerin waitress

kenmerk feature
kennen know
keramiek ceramics
kerk church
kerkdienst n service
ketel kettle
ketting chain
keuken kitchen
keukenpapier paper towel
kies v dial (phone)
kiespijn toothache
kijken v look
kilo kilo
kilometer kilometer
kind child
kinderarts pediatrician
kinderkleding children's clothing
kindermenu children's menu
kinderportie children's portion
kinderstoel highchair
kinderwagen stroller [pushchair BE]
kinderzitje car seat
kinderzwembad kiddie
   [paddling BE] pool
kiosk newsstand [news agent BE]
klaar ready
klanteninformatie
   customer information
klantenservice customer service
klas class
klederdracht costume (local)
kledingwinkel clothing store
klerenhanger coat hanger
klein small
klem clamp
kleur color
klier gland
klif cliff
kliniek clinic

klok clock
klomp n clog
klooster monastery
kloppen knock
kluis safe
knie knee
knippen v cut
knoop button
koekenpan frying pan
koel cool (temperature)
koelkast refrigerator
koerier courier
koffer suitcase
kok n cook
kom bowl
komen come
kookgelegenheid cooking facilities
koopje bargain
koorts fever
kopen buy
koper copper
kopie n photocopy
kopieerapparaat photocopier
kopiëren v photocopy
kopje cup
kort short
korte broek shorts
korting discount
koosjer kosher
kosten v cost
koud adj cold
kousen stockings
kraan faucet [tap BE]
kraanwater tap water
kramp cramps
krant newspaper
krap tight
krijgen get (receive)
kristal crystal

kroon crown (dental)
kruidenierswinkel grocery store [greengrocer BE]
kruier porter
kruis *n* cross
kruispunt intersection [junction BE]
krukken crutches
kwitantie receipt
kuil pothole (road)
kunnen *v* can
kunstenaar artist
kunstgalerie art gallery
kunstgebit denture
kurkentrekker corkscrew
kussen *n* pillow; *v* kiss
kust coast
kuuroord spa
kwaliteit quality
kwart quarter
kwijt missing

L

laag low
laantje lane
laarzen boots
laat late
laatste last
label label
lactose-intolerant lactose intolerant
ladder ladder
lager zetten turn down (volume, heat)
laken sheet
lamp lamp
land country
landen *v* land
landnummer country code
lang long
lange broek pants [trousers BE]
langzaam slow

laten zien show
lawaaierig noisy
laxerend middel laxative
ledikant cot
leeg *adj* empty (general); dead (battery)
leegmaken *v* empty
leer leather
legaal legal
legitimatiebewijs ID
lekken *v* leak
lekker delicious
lelijk ugly
lenen borrow (from); lend (to)
lengte height (person); length (general)
lens lens
lensdop lens cap
lepel spoon
leren learn
les lesson
leuk vinden enjoy
leunen lean
leven life
lever liver
levering delivery
lezen read
licht light
lichten headlights (car)
lichting collection (mail)
lid member
liefde *n* love
lift elevator [lift BE]
ligstoel deck chair
lijn line
limousine limousine
links left
linnen linen
lip lip
lippenstift lipstick
liter liter

logeren stay (overnight)
logies accommodations
logies-ontbijt bed and breakfast
lokaal local
loket ticket office
long lung
longontsteking pneumonia
loodvrij unleaded (gasoline)
lopen v walk
los loose
losschroeven unscrew
loterij lottery
lucht air
luchtbed air mattress
luchtpomp air pump
luchtpost airmail
luchtvaartmaatschappij airline
luchtziekte airsickness
lucifers matches
luid loud
luier diaper [nappy BE]
luik shutter
lunch lunch

M

maag stomach
maagpijn stomachache
maaltijd meal
maand month
maandverband sanitary napkin [pad BE]
maar but
maat size
maatbeker measuring cup
maatlepel measuring spoon
machine machine
magnetron microwave (oven)
magnifiek magnificent
maken make
make-up make-up

makkelijk easy
man man; husband
manager manager
mand basket
manicure manicure
mannelijk male
markt market
mascara mascara
masker mask
massage massage
matinee matinee
matras mattress
mededelingenbord bulletin board
medicijn medication
medische nooddienst emergency medical service
meedoen join
meegaan accompany (go with); last (keep)
meenemen v take
meer n lake; adj more
meisje girl
meneer Mr.
menstruatie period
menstruatiepijn menstrual cramps
menukaart menu
mes knife
met with
metaal metal
meten measure
metro subway [underground BE]
metrostation subway [underground BE] station
meubels furniture
Mevrouw Mrs.; madam
middag afternoon
middernacht midnight
migraine migraine
mijn mine

minder less
minibar mini-bar
minimum minimum
minuut minute
mis mass
misschien maybe
misselijk nauseous
misselijkheid nausea
mist fog
misverstand misunderstanding
mobiel cell [mobile BE] phone
modern contemporary
moe tired
moeilijk difficult
moeras swamp
moeten must
mogelijk possible
mogen v can
mok mug
molen windmill
mond mouth
monteur mechanic
mooi beautiful
morgen tomorrow
moskee mosque
motor engine
motorboot motorboat
motorfiets motorcycle
mountainbike mountain bike
mouw sleeve
muggenbeet mosquito bite
munt coin
museum museum
muur wall
muziek music

N

na after
naaien sew
naam n name

naar to
naast next to
nacht night
nachtapotheek all-night pharmacy
nachtclub night club
nagel nail
nagelsalon nail salon
nagelvijl nail file
nagesynchroniseerd dubbed
nat wet
nationaliteit nationality
natuur nature
natuurpad nature trail
natuurreservaat nature reserve
Nederlands Dutch (language)
Nederlanders Dutch (people)
nee no
neerzetten put
nek neck
nemen v take
netnummer area code
netwerk network
neus nose
niemand nobody
nier kidney
niet do not; not
niet-EU-ingezetenen
    non-EU-citizens
niet-roken non-smoking
niets nothing
nieuw new
nieuws news
Nieuw-Zeeland New Zealand
nodig necessary
nodig hebben need
nog adv still
non-stop non-stop
noodgeval emergency
noodrem emergency brake
nooduitgang emergency exit

nooit never
noord north
normaal normal; regular (gas)
nu now
nul zero
nummer number
nylon nylon

O

ochtend morning
of or
ogenblik moment
oké OK
olie oil
om at (time)
omdat because
omhelzen hug
omleiding detour [diversion BE]
onbeleefd rude
onbeperkt unlimited
onbevoegd unauthorized
onder under
ondertiteld subtitled
onderzoek examination
ondiep shallow
ongelijk uneven (ground)
ongelooflijk incredible
ongeluk accident
ongeveer about (approximately)
onschuldig innocent
ontbijt breakfast
ontdooien defrost
onthouden remember
ontmoeten meet
ontmoetingsplaats meeting place [point BE]
ontruimen vacate (room)
ontsteken infect
ontsteking inflammation
ontstopper plunger

onttrekken v extract
ontvangen receive
ontvangstcentrum reception center
ontwikkelen develop
ontwrichten dislocate
onvergezeld unaccompanied
onze our
onzin nonsense
oog eye
ook also
oom uncle
oor ear
oorbellen earrings
oordruppels ear drops
oorlogsmonument war memorial
oorpijn earache
oost east
op on
opdienen serve
open adj open
openbaar public
opendoen v open (window)
openen v open
openingstijden office hours
openlucht adj outdoor
openmaken open
opera opera
operatie operation
opgezet swollen
ophalen v pick up
oplossen dissolve
opnemen withdraw (money)
oppas babysitter
oppassen caution; beware
oprit entrance ramp (highway)
oproep call
opruiming clearance; sale
opslaan save (computer)
opstaan stand up
opstijgen take off (plane)

opvullen fill up
opticien optician
opwarmen v warm
organiseren organize
origineel original
orkest orchestra
oud old
oudere senior citizens
ouders parents
ovaal oval
oven oven
over about
overbagage excess luggage [baggage BE]
overdekt indoor
overgeven v vomit
overhemd shirt (men's)
overstappen v change (bus)
oversteken v cross
overtocht crossing

P

paar pair
paard horse
paardenrenbaan horsetrack
paardrijden horseback riding
paars purple
pad path
pak suit
pakket package [parcel BE]
paleis palace
panorama panorama
pantoffels slippers
paracetamol acetaminophen [paracetamol BE]
parasol umbrella (sun) [sunshade BE]
paraplu umbrella (rain)
parel pearl
park park
parkeer en reis park and ride

parkeerdienst valet service
parkeergarage parking garage [car park BE]
parkeermeter parking meter
parkeerplaats parking lot [car park BE]
parkeerplek parking space
parkeerbon parking ticket
parkeerverbod no parking
parkeren parking
particulier private
parttime part time
paskamer fitting room
paspoort passport
passagier passenger
passen try on (clothes)
patiënt n patient
pauze intermission
paviljoen pavilion
pech breakdown (car)
pedicure pedicure
pen pen
penicilline penicillin
pensioen retirement [pension BE]
pension guesthouse
per per
per expres express mail
periode period
persen v press
personeel staff
persoon person
picknick picnic
pijn n pain
pijn hebben v hurt
pijnlijk sore
pijp pipe
pil pill
PIN PIN
pincet tweezers
pizzeria pizzeria

plaats place (location); seat (on train, etc.)
plaatselijk local
plak slice
plan plan
plant *n* plant
planten *v* plant
plastic plastic
plat flat
platina platinum
plein square
pleister bandage [plaster BE]
plezier fun
plug plug
polikliniek health clinic
politie police
politiebureau police station
polyester polyester
pomp pump
pond pound
populair popular
porselein porcelain
portemonnee wallet
portie portion
post *n* mail
posten *v* mail
postkantoor post office
posttarief postage
postwissel money order
postzegel *n* stamp
pot pot
praktijk practice
praten talk
prepaidkaart prepaid phone card
pretpark amusement park
prijs price
prijsverlaging discount
prima fine (good)
primus kerosene stove
privé private

probleem problem
proces-verbaal police report
proeven *v* taste
programma program
proost cheers
pub pub
publiek public
pyjama pajamas

R

raam window
raadplegen consult
racket racket (tennis)
rapport report
reactie reaction
recept prescription
receptie reception
receptionist receptionist
recht straight
rechts right (direction)
rechtstreeks *adj* direct
reddingsboot life boat
reddingsgordel life preserver [belt BE]
reddingsvest life jacket
reduceren reduce
reformproducten health food
reformwinkel health food store
regen *n* rain
regenen v rain
regenjas raincoat
relatie relationship
reis trip
reisbureau travel agency
reischeque traveler's check [cheque BE]
reisgids tour guide
reisorganisator tour operator
reisziekte motion sickness [travel sickness BE]

reizen travel
rekening bill
rem brake
renbaan racetrack [race course BE]
rennen run
renovatie renovation
reparatie *n* repair
repareren *v* repair
reserveren *v* reserve
reservering reservation
reserveringsbalie reservation desk
reservoir reservoir
restaurant restaurant
restauratiewagen dining car (train)
retourtje round-trip [return BE] ticket
richting direction
riem belt
rietje straw
rij line [queue BE]
rijbaan lane
rijbewijs driver's license
rijden drive
rijstrook lane
ring ring
ritssluiting zipper
rivier river
roeiboot rowboat
roeien row
roestvrij staal stainless steel
route route
rok skirt
roken *v* smoke; smoking
    section (restaurant)
rokerszone smoking area
rolstoel wheelchair
rolstoelopgang wheelchair ramp
roltrap escalator
roman novel
romantisch romantic
rond round (shape); around

(direction)
rondleiding guided tour
rondvaart boat trip
röntgenfoto x-ray
roomservice room service
roos rose
rotonde traffic circle
    [roundabout BE]
rots rock
route route
roze pink
rug back (body part)
rugby rugby
rugpijn backache
rugzak backpack
ruilen exchange
ruimte space
rusten *v* rest
ruïne ruins
rustgebied rest area
rustig quiet

S

's avonds in the evening
's middags p.m.
's morgens a.m.
sms'en *v* text messaging
saai boring
sandalen sandals
satijn satin
sauna sauna
schaakspel chess
schaal scale
schaar scissors
schaatsen *n* skates; *v* ice-skating
schade damage
schadeclaim insurance claim
schaduw shade
schattig cute
scheerapparaat razor

scheerkwast shaving brush
scheermesje razor blade
scheerzeep shaving cream
scheiden divorce
schep shovel
scheren shave
scherp sharp
scheuren tear (muscle)
schilderij painting
schip ship
schoen shoe
schoenenwinkel shoe store
schoenmaker shoe repair
schok shock
schoon clean
schoonmaakmiddelen cleaning supplies
Schotland Scotland
schouder shoulder
schrijven write
schroevendraaier screwdriver
seks sex
selecteren choose
seminar seminar
servet napkin
shampoo shampoo
sieraden jewelry
siertegel decorative tile
sigaar cigar
sigarenwinkel tobacconist
sigaret cigarette
single single (person)
sjaal scarf
slaapkamer bedroom
slaappil sleeping pill
slaapwagen sleeping car
    [sleeper car BE]
slaapzak sleeping bag
slabbetje bib
slager butcher
slagveld battle site

slapeloosheid insomnia
slapen sleep
slecht bad
slechts only
slechthorend hearing impaired
slechtziend visually impaired
sleutel key
sleutelkaart key card
sleutelring key ring
slijter liquor store [off-licence BE]
slot n lock
sluiten v close
smaak n taste
smal narrow
smaragd emerald
snackbar snack bar
snel fast
snelheid speed
snelheidslimiet speed limit
snelweg highway [motorway BE]
sneeuw n snow
sneeuwen v snow
snijwond n cut
snoepwinkel candy store
    [confectioner BE]
snorkelen snorkle
sokken socks
soms sometimes
soort kind (type)
sorry sorry
soulmuziek soul music
souvenir souvenir
souvenirgids souvenir guide
souvenirwinkel souvenir store
spaarrekening savings account
spatel spatula
speciaal special
specialist specialist
speelgoed toy
speelgoedwinkel toy store

speelhal arcade
speeltuin playground
spelen play
spellen v spell
spelletje game
spiegel mirror
spier muscle
spijkerbroek jeans
spijkerstof denim
spitsuur rush hour
spons sponge
spoor platform
sport sport
sportwinkel sporting goods store
sportvereniging sports club
spreken speak
spreekkamer doctor's office
  [surgery BE]
spullen things
staal steel
staan stand
staanplaats standing room
stad town
stadhuis town hall
stadion stadium
stadscentrum downtown area
stadsplattegrond town map
stadsplein town square
standaard standard
standby-ticket stand-by ticket
starten v start
stadion stadium
standbeeld statue
station train [railway BE] station
steegje alley
steek bite (insect)
steelpan saucepan
steil steep
stelen steal
stempelen stamp

steriele oplossing sterilizing solution
sterk strong
sterling zilver sterling silver
steward flight attendant
stijf stiff
stijl n style
stilist stylist
stoep sidewalk [pavement BE]
stof fabric
stofzuiger vacuum cleaner
stomerij dry cleaner
stomen v steam
stopcontact electrical outlet
stoppen stop
stoplicht traffic light
storen disturb
straat street
strand beach
strandboulevard seafront
strandmeester lifeguard (beach)
streek region
strijken v iron
strijkijzer n iron
strippenkaart bus ticket
stroom stream (flow); electricity
  (power)
stroomversnelling rapids
stropdas n tie
student student
studeren study
stuifmeelgehalte pollen count
stuk piece
stylen v style
sufheid drowsiness
suikerpatiënt diabetic
sun-block sun-block cream
super premium (gas) [super BE]
supermarkt supermarket
surfplank surfboard
sweatshirt sweatshirt

symbool symbol
symptoom symptom
synagoge synagogue
synthetisch synthetic

T

T-shirt T-shirt
tv TV
taai tough
taalcursus language course
taalgids phrase book
tabak tobacco
tablet tablet
tafel table
takelwagen tow truck
tampon tampon
tand tooth
tandarts dentist
tandartspraktijk dental office
tandenborstel toothbrush
tandpasta toothpaste
tapijt carpet
tas bag
taxi taxi
taxistandplaats taxi stand [rank BE]
te too
team team
techniek engineering
teen toe
tegel tile
tegenover opposite
te kauwen chewable
tekenen v sign (signature)
te koop for sale
tekst n text
telefoneren v call (phone)
telefonist telephone operator
telefoon telephone
telefoongesprek phone call
telefoongids phone directory
telefoonkaart phone card

telefoonnummer phone number
telefoonzuil pay phone
temperatuur temperature
tenger petite
tenminste at least
tennis tennis
tennisbaan tennis court
tent tent
tentharing tent peg
tentstok tent pole
terminal terminal
terugbetaling refund n
terugbrengen v return (thing)
terugkomen v return (person)
terwijl while
theater theater
theelepel teaspoon
thermometer thermometer
thermosfles thermos
thuis home
tijd time
tijdschrift magazine
tin pewter
tint tint
tissue tissue
toebehoren belong
toegang access; admission
toegangsprijs admission charge
toestaan v permit
tourist tourist
toeristische rondrit sightseeing tour
toernooi tournament
toeslag surcharge
toestel extension (phone)
toezicht supervision
toilet restroom [toilet BE]
toiletpapier toilet paper
tol toll
tolhuisje toll booth
tolk interpreter

tolweg toll road
toneelstuk play (theater)
tonen v show
tong tongue
toren tower
tot until
touringcar long-distance bus
touw rope
traditioneel traditional
tram tram
trap stairs
trein train
trekken pull
trottoir sidewalk [pavement BE]
trouwen marry
trui sweater
tuin garden
tumor tumor
tunnel tunnel
tussen between
twaalf uur 's middags noon
    [midday BE]
tweedehandswinkel
    secondhand store
tweede klas economy class
tweepersoonskamer double room

U

u you (formal)
uit from (destination); out (general)
uitchecken check out
uitgaan go out
uitgids entertainment guide
uitgang n exit
uitgeput exhausted
uitgeven spend
uitgezonderd except
uitkijkpunt vantage point, overlook
uitkleden undress
uitloggen log off

uitnodigen v invite
uitrit exit
uitrusting equipment
uitslag rash
uitsluitend exclusively
uitspreken pronounce
uitstappen get off
uitstekend terrific
uitverkocht sold out
uitzetten turn off
uitzicht view
uur hour

V

vaak adv frequent
vacature vacancy
vakantie vacation [holiday BE]
vakantiehuisje cottage
valhelm helmet
vallei valley
vallen v fall
valuta currency
vanavond tonight
vandaag today
vasthouden v hold
vast menu fixed-price menu
vechten v fight
veerboot ferry
veganist vegan
vegen wipe, sweep (clean)
vegetariër n vegetarian
vegetarisch adj vegetarian
veilig safe
veiligheid safety
veiligheidsgordel seat belt
veiligheidsspeld safety pin
veilig voor kinderen childproof
veld field
ventilator n fan
ver far

verband bandage
verbazingwekkend amazing
verbeteren improve
verbinding connection
verbinding maken connect
verbinding verbreken disconnect
verboden prohibited
verboden toegang keep out
verbreken disconnect
verdieping floor (level in building)
verdovingsmiddel anesthetic
verdrinken drown
verdwaald lost
vereist required
Verenigde Staten U.S.
verf paint
vergadering meeting
vergaderruimte meeting room
vergeten forget
vergoeden v refund
vergoeding n refund
vergunning permit
vergroten enlarge
verhuizen move
verhuren rent out
verjaardag birthday
verkeerd wrong
verkeer traffic
verkeersovertreding traffic violation
  [offence BE]
verkeersvrij gebied pedestrian zone
  [precinct BE]
verklaring statement
verkoop sale
verkopen sell
verkoudheid cold (flu)
verkrachting rape
verlamming paralysis
verliezen lose
verloofd engaged (marriage)

verloofde fiance
verloren lost
vermaken alter
verminderen reduce
verontschuldigen apologize
verpleegster nurse
verplicht mandatory
verrekken strain (muscle)
verrekijker binoculars
vers fresh
verschonen change (baby)
verschuldigd zijn owe
versie version
versnapering refreshment
versnelling gear
versperd blocked
verstellen mend (clothes)
verstopt blocked
verstuiken twist (ankle)
versturen send (general); mail (mail)
vertalen translate
vertaler translator
vertaling translation
vertellen tell
vertraagd delayed
vertraging delay
vertrek departures (airport)
vertrekgate departure gate
vertrekken v leave
vervaldatum expiration [expiry BE] date
vervangen replace
vervangingsonderdeel
replacement part
vervelend unpleasant
verven v paint
vervoer transport
verwarming heat [heating BE]
verwijderen remove (general);
  delete (computer)
verwonden injure

verzekering insurance
verzekeringsbewijs insurance card
  [certificate BE]
verziend far-sighted
  [long-sighted BE]
videospelletje video game
vierkant square
vies dirty
vijver pond
vinden find
vinger finger
vissen fishing
visitekaartje business card
visum visa
vitrine display case
vlek stain
vlieg *n* fly
vliegen *v* fly
vliegtuig airplane
vliegveld airport
vlo flea
vlooienmarkt flea market
vlucht flight
vluchtinformatie flight information
vluchtnummer flight number
vochtig damp
vochtinbrengende crème
  moisturizer
voeden feed
voedsel food
voedselvergiftiging food poisoning
voelen feel
voertuig vehicle
voet foot
voetbal soccer [football BE]
voetganger pedestrian
voetgangersgebied traffic-free zone
voetgangersoversteekplaats
  pedestrian crossing
voetpad footpath

vogel bird
vol full
volgen follow
volgende next
volleybal volleyball
voltage voltage
volwassene adult
voor before (time)
voorbeeld example
voorbehoedsmiddel contraceptive
voordat before
voorkant front
voorrang right of way
voorrang verlenen yield
  [give way BE]
voorruit windshield [windscreen BE]
voorstellen introduce (person);
  suggest (subject)
voorstelling performance
voortreffelijk superb
voorzichtig careful
vorige adj last
vork fork
vorm shape
vrachtwagen truck [lorry BE]
vragen ask
vreemd strange
vreselijk terrible
vriend friend (male); boyfriend
vriendelijk friendly
vriendin friend (female); girlfriend
vrij free (no charge); vacant
  (unoccupied)
vroeg early
vrouw woman; wife
vrouwelijk female
vuilnis trash [rubbish BE]
vuilniszak trash bag
vullen fill
vulling filling

vuur fire
vuurtoren lighthouse
VVV tourist office

W

waar where (location); true (accurate)
waarde value
waardevol valuable
waarschuwing warning
wachten wait
wachtkamer waiting room
wachtwoord password
wagentje cart [trolley BE]
wagon car
wakker maken wake (someone)
Wales Wales
wandelen walking (general); hiking (on trail)
wandelpad walkway; trail (nature)
wandelroute walking route
wandeluitrusting hiking gear
wanneer when
warenhuis department store
warme bron hot spring
wasbaar washable
wasknijper peg
wasmachine washing machine
wasmiddel detergent
wassen wash
wasserette laundromat [launderette BE]
wasserij laundry service
wastafel sink
wat what
water water
waterski's water skis
waterskiën waterskiing
waterdicht waterproof
waterval waterfall

wedden bet
wedstrijd contest (general); game (sport)
weduwe widowed (female)
weduwnaar widowed (male)
week week
weekdag weekday
weekend weekend
weekendtarief weekend rate
weer weather
weerbericht weather forecast
weg n road; adv away
wegen weigh
wegenkaart road map
wegwerpbaar disposable
weiland field
weinig few
wekdienst wake-up call service
wekker alarm clock
welke which
welkom welcome
wenkbrauw eyebrow
wens wish
werk n work
werkeloos unemployed
werken v work
wesp wasp
west west
wie who
wieg crib [child's cot BE]
wielerwedstrijd cycling race
wielklem clamp
wij we
wijngaard vineyard
wijnkaart wine list
wijnproeven wine tasting
wijzigen v change
wind wind
winderig windy

windjack windbreaker
windmolen windmill
windsurfen windsurfing
winkel store
winkelbediende shop assistant
winkelcentrum shopping mall
    [centre BE]
winkelen v shopping
winkelmandje shopping basket
winkelplattegrond store guide
    [directory BE]
winkelwagentje shopping cart
    [trolley BE]
wisselen exchange
wisselgeld change
wisselkantoor currency exchange office
wisselkoers exchange rate
wit white
wol wool
wonen live
woonerf residential zone
woordenboek dictionary
worden become

Z

zakdoek handkerchief
zaken business
zakencentrum business district
zaklantaarn flashlight [torch BE]
zand sand
zebrapad crosswalk
[zebra crossing BE]
zee sea
zeep soap
zeespiegel sea level
zeeziek seasick
zeggen say
zekeringkast fuse box
zeldzaam rare
zeker sure

zelfbediening self-service
zelfgemaakt homemade
zelfstandig self-employed
zetpil suppository
ziek sick [ill BE]
ziekenhuis hospital
ziektekostenverzekeing
    health insurance
zien see
zijde silk
zilver silver
zinsnede phrase
zitplaats seat
zitten sit
zoet sweet
zon sun
zonder without
zonnebaden sunbathe
zonnebrand sunburn
zonnebrandcrème sunscreen
zonnebril sunglasses
zonnesteek sunstroke
zout n salt; adj salty
zuid south
zuigfles baby bottle
zuivel dairy
zuivelproducten dairy products
zuiver pure
zuurstof oxygen
zwaar heavy
zwanger pregnant
zwelling swelling
zwembad swimming pool
zwembroek swimming trunks
zwemmen swimming
zwempak swimsuit
zwemvest life jacket